ALL HER GLORIES PAST

All Her Glories Past

The Story of the Zetland Lifeboat

David Phillipson

First published in 1994 by

Smith Settle Ltd
Ilkley Road
Otley
West Yorkshire
LS21 3JP

ISBN Paperback 1 85825 024 2

British Library Cataloguing-in-Publication Data:
A catalogue record is available for this book
from the British Library.

Designed, printed and bound by
SMITH SETTLE
Ilkley Road, Otley, West Yorkshire LS21 3JP

Contents

Acknowledgments

It is difficult to live in Redcar and not be aware of the *Zetland*. As a boy I often peered with curiosity through the boathouse windows at the old boat. The close association I formed with it in later years I owe entirely to my mother. She was secretary of the Ladies Lifeboat Guild during the period between 1961 and 1969, when members of the guild opened the boathouse on weekends and special occasions during the summer to raise funds for the RNLI. We spent many happy hours selling souvenirs and caring for the boat and boathouse. Later still I was employed by Langbaurgh Borough Council in the extensive museum that had been created around the *Zetland*.

It would not have been possible to compile such a complete story of the *Zetland* without the invaluable research and support of my partner Jane Foreman. From hundreds of hours spent reading old documents and newspapers she has discovered a wealth of information that had long been forgotten. Her work has added an incredible amount to what was already known about the *Zetland* and has enhanced the story of the boat that has given Redcar a place in history.

A special thanks must go to Phil Philo, curator of Kirkleatham Old Hall Museum, for his encouragement and enthusiasm, and for permission to use photographs from the museum collection.

I would like also to express my gratitude to the following for their valuable assistance:

Mr A E Edwards, a member of the Redcar Lifeboat Management Committee, and custodian on their behalf of the *Journal of Shipwrecks* kept by John and Stephen Coulson, the Journal of Peter Walton, and a copy of the correspondence regarding the loss of the *Belsay Castle*.

Mr J Carr, of Redcar, former headmaster of Zetland School, for allowing access to the school log books.

Private collectors who made available the letter regarding the loss of the *Arcturus*, postcards for illustrations and the Whitby Repository.

Mr F W J Morris, retired station officer of coastguard, for providing details on the naval career of Lt R E Pym.

The late Mr T Parratt, whose extensive records of the history of Redcar greatly assisted research into the career of the *Zetland* after her retirement.

I am also most grateful to the staffs of the following organisations for their co-operation and enthusiasm:

RNLI Headquarters, Poole, and in particular Barry Cox, honorary librarian, and Joan Davies, editor of *The Lifeboat* between 1976 and 1984.

The reference libraries at Middlesbrough, Newcastle, North Shields, Redcar, South Shields and York.

The Bodleian Library, Oxford.

Hartlepool Maritime Museum.

Cleveland County Archives.

Tees and Hartlepool Port Authority.

David Phillipson
Redcar   1994

1802-1809

There was much excitement in the North Yorkshire village of Redcar during the summer of 1802. In the neat, whitewashed houses, all but buried by wind-blown sand, the talk was all of the new lifeboat. It was to be built by a South Shields boatbuilder named Henry Greathead. He had been commissioned to build his first lifeboat in 1789 and it had proved to be such a success that further orders had quickly followed. Greathead was invited to visit various ports and give lectures on the advantages of his lifeboats. At Whitby, in July 1802, he was instructed to build a lifeboat for Redcar. His order book shows that the request came from the Rt Hon Lord Thomas Dundas, and the Rev Thomas Pym Williamson.

Lord Dundas owned considerable estates in the Cleveland area and many Redcar families were his tenants. He was a benevolent landlord who concerned himself with the welfare of the communities dependant upon him. He was also no stranger to the hazards of the coast. A laden sloop owned by him had been wrecked on the rocks off Redcar in February, 1802. Fortunately all on board were saved.

The Dundas country residence was at Upleatham, a few miles inland from Redcar, and in the parish of Guisborough, where the Rev Thomas Pym Williamson was vicar.

At the time the order for the lifeboat was placed, the geography of the Tees estuary differed greatly from today. For more than seven miles the German Ocean washed on a broad swathe of desolate, windswept sand. From the ancient walled town of Hartlepool, the golden expanse curved past the village of Seaton Carew, broke for the shallow, shifting entrance of the Tees, then swept on past the villages of Coatham, Redcar, and Marske. At Saltburn it ended abruptly at the lonely Ship Inn under the shadow of Huntcliffe.

The principal port of the Tees was Stockton, about ten miles up the winding course of the river. Although the tidal reaches were difficult to navigate they held none of the hazards of the passage over the bar. The estuary extended from Todd Point, about two miles north of Redcar, to a similar distance south of

A lithograph of Redcar around the mid-nineteenth century by John Jordison. Far left is St Peters Church. Amongst those buried in the churchyard is William Guy, lost from the Zetland on Christmas day 1836. Next to the church is Redcar windmill, home of Stephen Coulson in 1838. Far right is Coatham windmill where Robert Coulson was miller. He was the brother with whom Stephen exchanged heated letters, published in York newspapers, over the loss of some of the crew of the brig Belsay Castle. (Photograph by courtesy of Kirkleatham Old Hall Museum.)

Seaton Carew. Two triangular sandbanks, known as the North and South Gares, flanked the mouth of the river. Variations in wind direction caused the sand to shift constantly, and the direction of the main channel varied considerably.

To the south of the Tees the sand drifted into high dunes that formed a natural defence against the sea. Behind them flat agricultural land extended to the wooded hills that hid Guisborough, the one-time capital of Cleveland. From Redcar, broad fingers of rock reach out from the shore for more than a mile. At high water they are completely covered and at low water are exposed to a height of up to 8 feet (2.4 metres) and form a natural harbour. It was haven to a small fleet of cobles, the traditional lean, high-prowed vessels of the North-East coast. Hardy men from Redcar and Coatham won a precarious livelihood from fishing, or as pilots that ranged far to seaward to seek Teesbound ships.

The new lifeboat was ready by October 1802 and details of its arrival were given in the *Newcastle Courant* for the 16th of that month. (The following extracts are from a letter from Guisborough, respecting the lifeboat.)

The Zetland *in front of South Terrace, better known in Redcar as Fishermans Square because of the generations of fishing families that have lived there. The photograph was taken by T W Bainbridge. (From a postcard in a private collection.)*

'We have the pleasure to inform our readers that a lifeboat built by Mr. Greathead of South Shields is now established at Redcar on the Yorkshire coast. It arrived on this station on the 7th inst., and was received with great joy by the inhabitants of that place, who vied with each other, in expressing their gratitude to a benevolent public who so graciously subscribed towards the accomplishment of so humane an Institution.

In the evening the fishermen were regaled with ale to drink success to the boat and the health of the builder, who by this happy invention has added a most valuable treasure to this nation generally, and to the honest and brave race of men who are its chief pillar in particular. We are happy to add that the fishermen unanimously and in the most voluntary and heartfelt manner declared "she should never want hands to man her when called for".'

Other accounts record that the lifeboat was brought from Shields 'by pilots of that place' and that there had been 'a house erected for its receipt by Rt. Hon. Ld. Dundas'.

Greathead provided clear instructions as to how his lifeboats should be used to achieve maximum success.

'These boats are built of two sizes, one to row with ten oars, the other with eight, for the conveniency of those places where a larger number of hands

3

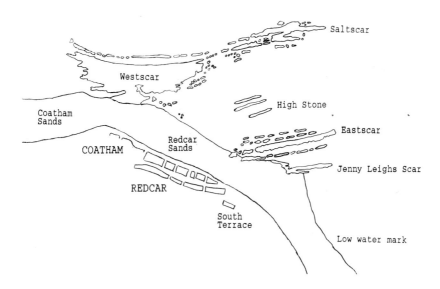

A map of Redcar rocks. Scar is from the old Norse word sker, *meaning bare craggy rocks.*

cannot on the sudden be obtained. Each of these boats require two men besides the rowers, who ought to be acquainted with the sets of the tides where the boat is likely to be used; these are to station themselves, one at each end of the boat, equipped with a long sweep, for the purpose of steering; for by the boat being fore and aft perfectly similar, she rows and steers either way with ease; he as to whom the rowers face, becomes steersman; the other must be very careful to keep his sweep out of the water. The rowers row double banked, with their oars slung over an iron thole provided with a grommet, which enables the rowers, merely by facing about, to row either way without turning the boat, a circumstance of infinite importance in broken water.

In going to a wreck, if more than one point of land from which to send the boat can be obtained, it will be found advisable to launch her so that she may head the sea as much as possible; the steersman must keep his eye fixed upon the waves or breakers, and encourage the rowers to give way to the boat as she rises to them; the boat thus aided by the force of the oars, launches over the waves with great rapidity, without shipping any water. It is necessary here to observe, that there is often a strong reflux of sea near stranded vessels, which requires both dispatch and care in the persons employed, that the boat be not damaged by striking the wreck. In returning from the wreck, should the wind

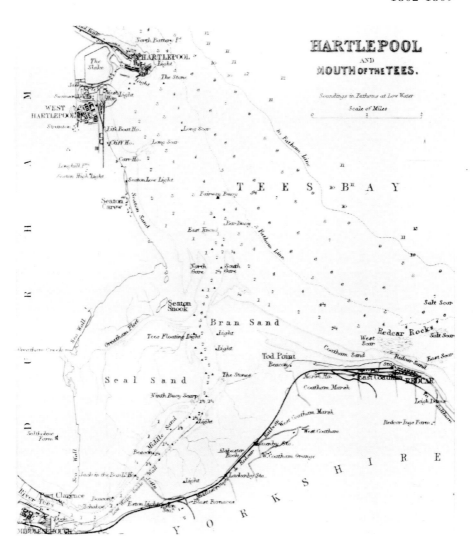

A chart of the Tees estuary about 1860. From Eston station the line of the
Middlesbrough to Redcar railway ran along the south bank of the river for a
considerable distance. The channel between the North and South Gare
sandbanks is shown as having as little as a fathom (6 feet or 1.83m) at low
water. Despite the difficulties created by not being able to enter at all states
of the tide, almost 4,000 ships visited the Tees in 1860. The chart, which
would seem to have been produced by A Fullarton and Company of London
and Edinburgh, is in the collection of Kirkleatham Old Hall Museum.

blow toward the land, the boat will come on shore without any effort than of steering.

These boats are painted white on the outside, this colour more immediately relieving the eye of the spectator at their rising from the hollow of the sea, than any other; the bottom is first varnished for the more minute inspection of purchasers, but it may be painted afterwards if preferred. The oars which the boat is provided with, are made of fir of the best quality, as it has been found by experience that a rove ash oar, that will dress clean and light, is too pliant among the breakers, and, if it be made strong and heavy, the rowers are sooner exhausted, as the purchase is necessarily short, from their rowing double banked; this circumstance makes the fir oar, when made stiff, much to be preferred: she is also furnished with puoys or sets, being better calculated than boat hooks to push off from soft sand among the breakers. [A puoy was a pole used to propel a boat in shallows or push it off into deeper water.]

These boats have also, when situation renders it necessary, a carriage or truck for the purpose of transporting them from their boathouse to the point of land nearest the wreck, or where they will be able to head the sea most directly. The rollers of the trucks are made concave, for the purpose of rolling them over spars or oaks laid lengthways on the sand, if it should not be sufficiently hard to bear the weight of the boat.

N.B. I would strongly recommend practising the boat in rough weather; by which means experience will be gained, and the danger become less, from the well-grounded confidence the people will have in the boat. It may perhaps be of some utility to post these instructions in conspicuous places, for the perusal of such persons as are likely to be employed in the boat.'

(signed) Henry Greathead. South Shields, 4th June 1803.

Greathead's lifeboats had a cork lining, 12 inches (30 cm) thick, that reached from the deck to the underside of the thwarts along either side. Beneath the gunwale on the outside a cork fender, 4 inches (10 cm) wide, extended downwards for 16 inches (40 cm). It was 21 feet (6.4 m) long and reached to within 4½ inches (11 cm) of the stem and stern. The vessels were built of oak reputedly seasoned for twenty years and had no means of freeing themselves of water other than bailing. Neither would they right themselves in the event of being capsized. The lifeboat sent to Redcar was of the larger type and measured approximately 30 feet (9.1m) in length by 10 feet (3.0m) in the beam.

In less than two months after its arrival the new lifeboat had made its first rescue. The event was described in a letter to the *Newcastle Chronicle* from the Rev William Leigh Williamson, father of Thomas Pym Williamson.

'11th December, 1802

"Ship News"

We are happy in the opportunity of recording another remarkable instance of the great utility of Life-Boats in preserving the lives of our fellow creatures.

The Zetland outside Marske Hall on her journey back to Redcar in 1906. (See also page 96.) Marske Hall had been the home of the Dundas family and later Henry Walker Yeoman, all great benefactors of the Zetland. Those on board are believed to be: Pearson Jackson, Thomas Hood Picknett, John Picknett, George Picknett, Thomas Maude Picknett, Thomas Stonehouse and 'Whisper' Picknett. (Photograph by courtesy of Kirkleatham Old Hall Museum.)

In the afternoon of yesterday se'nnight (5th Dec) the crews of 2 ships (the *Friendship*, Capt. Gilbert Shotton, of Newcastle, 9 men, and the *Sarah*, Capt. John Williamson, of Sunderland, 6 men) were saved near the mouth of the Tees, by Redcar Life-boat.

The distress was no sooner perceived at Redcar, than every inhabitant was in motion. Without waiting for the assistance of horses, they flew to the Boat-house and drew out the Boat, which they hurried away with such rapidity that they had nearly reached the place of launching (about 3 miles off) before they were overtaken by the horses.

The larger ship disappeared soon after the crew were brought off, and what became of the other is yet uncertain. About 25 fishermen were concerned in this very spirited and humane undertaking.

The Redcar people are so fond of the Boat that they say she is worth her

7

weight in gold. We beg leave to suggest the expediency of every ship having a gun on board, to give signal of distress in similar cases; for had the above accident happened at night, every soul on board must have perished. The Life-Boat was lately sent to Redcar, and built at South Shields, by Mr. Greathead,-

"Whose name shall ever live renown'd,
alike to Fame and Albion dear;
Whilst commerce spreads her sails around
Whilst British Tars the World revere:
To latest ages still it shall descend,
grac'd with the title of the Sailors Friend.'"

1803 - 1809

Few details have survived of the early rescues made by the lifeboat at Redcar. This may be due in part to the village being relatively isolated and its inhabitants of necessity being practical and self-reliant. Fishing was the principal occupation and the extra hazard of manning the lifeboat was probably accepted philosophically by men used to the ways of the sea. They were men of action not scholars, and would not have given thought to keeping a record of their deeds of heroism.

That any information has survived at all is thanks largely to John and Stephen Coulson, who kept a journal of shipwrecks at Redcar between September 1825 and October 1858. The journal was continued to July 1888 by a copy of records kept by William Picknett, and an unknown hand furnished the details between April 1801 and September 1825.

In 1821 T Jennet, of Stockton, published an eight page pamphlet entitled *Extract of a Journal Kept on the Coast of Redcar from the Year 1800 - 1819*, by Peter Walton, an officer in the Customs stationed at Redcar. It provides additional information on some of the shipwrecks recorded by John and Stephen Coulson and makes reference to one or two not listed by them.

The Local Records of Stockton and the Neighbourhood, by Thomas Richmond, also contain a number of references to the Redcar lifeboat. The book was originally published in 1868 and re-printed by Patrick and Shotton in 1972.

From time to time the details from these three sources are in dispute and for this reason all variances are included.

1804

About midnight on 8th March the inhabitants of Redcar were startled by the sound of gunfire. They feared that the French were off the coast and drums were beaten to alert the militia, or Sea Fencibles. They quickly assembled on the sands under the command of Captain Thrush.

It was discovered that the brig *Rose*, of London, Captain Sibbold (or Seffald), had run aground on the rocks and was firing minute guns to attract attention. The lifeboat was launched but failed to reach the vessel; this was possibly because there was not a sufficient depth of water to get alongside. The twenty-six men on board were eventually brought ashore by fishing boats. The brig became a total wreck although her cargo of timber was saved.

The alarm shown by the people of Redcar was understandable as there was a very real fear of invasion by the French. The village was on the edge of the sea and consisted of about 160 houses built either side of a single street. About 400 yards (366 metres) along the shore towards the Tees was the smaller village of Coatham. The rumble of surf frequently formed a background to conversation, even indoors. A few farms were scattered about the area and the nearest villages

Waves breaking against Redcar Esplanade photographed from Redcar pier. Through the spray, boats can be seen parked along the roadside out of reach of the sea. The square-topped building on the right is the boathouse built for the Free Gardeners *lifeboat. (From a postcard in a private collection.)*

were about three miles distant. Except for the glimmer of breakers along the shore, the darkness of a winter's night would have been complete.

On the 29th October the brig *Mary*, of Shields, in ballast, captain Worth (or North), was wrecked on Saltscar. A London brig, captain Heck, went on shore near Marske. Both crews were saved by Redcar lifeboat.

1807

30th January (or June). A sloop from Newcastle for Stockton, Mowbray master, was stranded in an attempt to enter the Tees. Two men who assisted to unload her cargo were rendered incapable by grog and were drowned when the tide flowed over the vessel. The others on board were saved by Redcar lifeboat. Accounts differ as to whether they were 8 or 15 in number.

11th November. The *Endeavour*, of Whitby, was wrecked on the South Gare and her crew drowned. The *Farmers Increase*, of Whitby, and the *Brunton* were wrecked at Coatham, and the *Peggy*, of Ipswich, was wrecked at Redcar. Their crews, who numbered 5, 6 and 6 respectively, were saved by Redcar lifeboat. There were also 2 vessels ashore at Marske.

23rd November. During a severe storm at least 17 vessels were driven ashore between the Tees and Sunderland. The brig *Ant*, of Lynn, Maxim captain, with corn for Newcastle, was lost at Coatham. The crew were saved by Redcar lifeboat.

In his book *A Trip to Coatham*, published in 1810, William Hutton recorded:

'In November last, a vessel laden with barley from Lynn, bound for the North, was wrecked; and when the tide was down, the sands were strewed with barley. The peasantry assembled; when the tide served, large quantities were recovered.

In the beginning of last month (September 1808), they had found the spot where the vessel went to pieces. If they had only got the shell before, they now found the yolk; for, by digging half a yard into the sand, I saw them recover many bushels, black as ink, and was told they acquired more than one hundred bushels. About a dozen people laboured three or four recesses of the tide.'

23rd December. The *Mary Ann*, of Yarmouth, laden with coal, was lost on Saltscar. The crew were saved by Redcar lifeboat.

1808

20th March. The sloop *Newbiggin*, of Whitby, Ness captain, stranded on the North Gare. All hands saved by Redcar lifeboat.

26th March. A strong gale blew from the east and a very heavy sea was running. For ten days the smack *Caledonia* had beaten against it in an effort to reach London from her home port of Aberdeen.

On board were a number of passengers and a valuable cargo of fifty tons of hewn granite, salmon fresh and kitted, pickled cod fish in casks, bales of linen, yarn thread, stockings, and great quantities of plate and other goods.

As darkness came the *Caledonia* stood in toward the land after a change of tack and at about 11 o'clock struck Saltscar. Only the helmsman was on deck at the time, the others being asleep below. He awoke them and a signal of distress was fired. It was not heard on shore and although the captain was urged to fire another he at first refused. As the danger increased he relented but by that time the powder had got wet.

It was two hours after low water and as the flood tide advanced the sea grew heavier. The granite in the smack prevented her rising to beat over the rocks. She left her bottom where she had first struck and her upper part drove to Westscar. Her mast broke and went away. When she started to break up, several ventured off in the ship's boat but it was capsized and they were lost.

In the morning the wreck was seen from the shore. The lifeboat was launched and with great difficulty those that had survived the dreadful night were rescued. They had lashed themselves in the rigging to be above the waves. Two of their number had drowned or died from exposure and were found entangled in the ropes.

The account of the tragedy is based on details in a notebook kept by John Agar, collector of duties of anchorage, groundage, and beaconage for Charles Turner. He records the smack as being two years old and of 130 tons.

Accounts differ as to whether 17 of those on board were lost and 6 saved, or 16 lost and 7 saved. Perhaps some reliance can be put on the Marine Intelligence column of the *Newcastle Courant* of the 2nd April 1808. It recorded that of 14 passengers only 4 were saved and of 9 seamen only 2 were saved. The name of the captain was given as Horley.

One body was found on the 27th March, and six more at Redcar and one at Coatham on the 29th. Included amongst the latter was a West India captain named John Booth.

In *A Trip to Coatham* William Hutton recalled that ten bodies were 'brought and laid upon a bench at the Red Lion (Hotel) Redcar; those of the other six were never found.

Their friends were written to; two gentlemen came from Aberdeen, ordered their funerals, and discharged the expenses. They now lie in Marske churchyard.

Melancholy curiosity induced me to visit their tombs. They lie five in a row, a good yard and a half asunder; and four feet below them lie the other five in the same order; two of them have head stones.' (Captain Booth and John Burnett.)

The funerals are recorded in the burial register: 30th March, Captain John Booth, age 50 (or 63); Captain William Heley, of the smack *Caledonia*; Joseph S - , mate; James Mackie, seaman; J.Rumey (Runsey?), seaman; William

Philips, seaman; Andrew Creig, seaman. 4th April, John Mather, passenger, age 50; Thomas Henry, passenger, age 30; John Burnett, passenger, age 18.

Hutton wrote that at the time of the shipwreck 'the whole crew were asleep, except the man upon the watch, who, not apprehending danger, was unwilling to disturb them'. He goes on to censure the captain and crew for the loss of life.

After a walk on the sands he commented 'I saw two hundred pieces of her timber; one was part of a mast 50 feet (15 metres) long, which now lies in the sands, but it is sold for six pounds'.

It is said that portions of granite from the cargo of the *Caledonia* were used to pave the footpaths of Moore Street, Redcar, and were not removed until 1890.

29th December. The Swedish brig *Magdelina*, laden with wine and salt, was lost on the North Gare. All hands were saved by Redcar lifeboat.

1809

25th November, Marine Intelligence, *Newcastle Courant*.

'In a heavy gale of Saturday a.m. last (18th) the *Fanny*, Smithson master, of Scarborough together with another vessel supposed to be the *Friends* (later corrected to *Generous Friends*) of Scarborough, in attempting to enter the river Tees struck on the North Gare and immediately went to pieces. The crews unfortunately all perished. The body of a lady - well dressed -who was a passenger in one of the vessels has since been washed on shore. It appears by some papers found on her that her name is Sarah Linskill belonging to Scarborough.

The *Edward*, Wealand master, of Dover, and the *Neptune*, Stephens master, of Scarborough, ran ashore at the same time near the Tees Mouth and are likely to become wrecks. Crews all saved by the providential assistance of the Redcar lifeboat.

The *Doves Escursion*, Hewitt master, of Wisbeach, is on shore near Marske. Her coals are landed and it is expected she will be got off. About 30 more loaded colliers got into the Tees - many of them considerably damaged and cannot proceed on their voyages till repaired.'

The journal kept by Peter Walton recorded the wind as north-east and that the lifeboat took three men out of the rigging of the *Neptune* and eight out of the *Edward*. The *Neptune* was later got off by Redcar fishermen.

1810-1819

1810

Redcar had grown in popularity as a resort and boasted twelve bathing-machines. No doubt visitors from inland viewed the lifeboat as an interesting curiosity and made donations towards its upkeep.

From *The Local Records of Stockton and the Neighbourhood*, by Thomas Richmond.

'18th September. The opening of the cut or canal between Stockton and Portrack took place, with great rejoicings. The morning was ushered in by the ringing of bells. At half-past seven, 3 sloops, decorated with flags, proceeded from Portrack through the cut, attended by the Volunteer band of music, the custom-house boat, the Redcar life-boat, and a number of pleasure boats etc; guns were fired from the vessels as they entered into and went out of the canal, which were answered by guns placed on the quays at Stockton.

When the sloops arrived at the Custom-house Quay, the company's flag was taken from the mast-head of the first sloop, and conveyed through the street, preceded by the band of music, and placed on the top of the cupola at the Town Hall. At 12 o'clock, the workmen employed in the cut, and the rowers of the Redcar life-boat etc., were regaled with beef and porter; and at 2 p.m., 72 gentlemen sat down to an excellent dinner at the Town Hall, the Volunteer band playing at intervals during the time.'

1814

8th (or 14th) October. The sloop *Two Brothers*, of Stockton (or Whitby), Cooper captain (or John Hall), from Sunderland with coal, was wrecked on the South Gare. Her crew of seven were saved by Redcar lifeboat.

1815

27th January. A brig of Boston, laden with coal, was wrecked on the South (or North) Gare. Six were saved by Redcar lifeboat. The wind was north east and stormy.

7th December. The brig *Freedom*, of Yarmouth, laden with coal, was wrecked on the North Gare. The master was saved but the other seven on board were lost. The journal kept by Peter Walton recorded that the Redcar lifeboat was out all night. The wind was from the north-east and very stormy.

1817

15th November. The sloop *Rifleman*, of Portsmouth, Smith master, laden with coal, was wrecked on Saltscar. The journals of John and Stephen Coulson, and Peter Walton, recorded that the crew of nine were saved by Redcar lifeboat but there would seem to be some doubt. The Marine Intelligence column of the *Newcastle Courant* stated that the crew took to their own boat and landed at Hartlepool. The hull and the cargo of the *Rifleman* were later sold for £59.

19th December. During a storm from the north-east, six Redcar fishermen in two boats were saved by Redcar lifeboat.

1819

27th January. Six fishermen were saved by Redcar lifeboat from two boats returning to Redcar with fish. The wind was south-east.

16th (or 6th) April. Six fishermen were saved by Redcar lifeboat from two Redcar fishing boats. The wind was north-east and the weather stormy.

31st December. Three fishermen were saved by Redcar lifeboat from a fishing boat returning to Redcar with fish. The wind was north-west.

1820-1829

1820

Thomas Dundas died on 14th June in his eightieth year. He had been created Baron Dundas of Aske in 1794. In 1802 he and the Rev Thomas Pym Williamson had placed the order with Henry Greathead for the lifeboat at Redcar. Lord Dundas was succeeded by his son, Lawrence.

1822

13th October. The brig *Ovington*, of Newcastle, captain Waters, was wrecked on Marske sand. The wind was north-east and the weather very stormy. The thirteen people on board were rescued by a coble but one died later.

The *Book of the Lifeboat* (1894) contains several accounts of shipwrecks recorded in dialect. They were the recollections of Jackie Stonehouse, who at the time he was interviewed was in his eighty-seventh year and the oldest fisherman in Redcar.

He remembered how waves had broken so heavily over the *Ovington* that at times she had been hidden from sight. Those watching had thought it impossible that anyone on board could be alive.

At dusk she had been close to rocks with both anchors down on eighty fathoms (146 metres) of chain. The foremast had been cut away and later the top of the mainmast was taken off in an effort to reduce resistance to the storm. As night closed in, the anchors began to drag. It was certain that the brig would come ashore but difficult to predict the exact spot. Ten men were paid five shillings (25p) each to watch for her and the 'drum went about for the lifeboat'.

By good fortune the brig was carried clear of the rocks and struck below Red Howles, midway between Redcar and Marske. She washed right up the sands and lay broadside to the breakers. There was barely enough water for the lifeboat so a coble was launched in the lee of the wreck. The rescuers found those on board in a pitiful state. An eighteen year old man was all but dead from

15

Redcar fisherman Jackie Stonehouse, aged eighty-seven, on Eastscar. His reminiscences, recounted in dialect, appeared in The Book of the Lifeboat, *published in 1894. They provide exciting eyewitness accounts on the early career of the* Zetland *that might otherwise have been recorded in only a few brief details. (Photograph by courtesy of Kirkleatham Old Hall Museum.)*

exposure and two women were found up to their chins in water in a cabin and in a very distressed condition. They had been to London to meet their husbands and were returning to Sunderland.

After their rescue they were wrapped in coats given by two men from Marske and taken to the Crown and Anchor Inn at Redcar. The young man was also taken there but all efforts to revive him failed.

It would seem to be the first reference to a drum being used to summon the lifeboat crew. The method was used until the close of the century and possibly had its origins in the Napoleonic wars when a drum was beaten to assemble the local militia. (As occurred in the incident of the brig *Rose* in March 1804.) The urgent signal beaten for the lifeboat crew is popularly believed to have been to the rhythm of 'Come along brave boys, come along!'

The *Ovington* had been bound from London to Newcastle with a general cargo valued at £40,000. The hull was later sold for £130. Jackie Stonehouse recalled that the cargo included hundreds of cheeses and that for six weeks men were employed in taking them to the Tees and loading them onto three sloops.

William Ward Jackson, of Normanby Hall, was a conscientious diarist and one of his entries contains an interesting reference to the lifeboat:

'Sunday 13th October. Storm and rain all day. Monday 14th October. Edwin [his fifteen year old son] rode down to Redcar. 5 light colliers came on shore yesterday on West Coatham sands. Newcastle trade - beyond Redcar. No hands drowned, but one or two finished by cold. The lifeboat was launched and went down, (being worn out) with 20 men in it, fortunately just after leaving land, and all got on shore.'

The five light colliers were brigs and were in addition to the *Ovington*. Two are recorded as being got off later.

That the lifeboat was 'worn out' is hardly surprising considering its arduous career. A few of Greathead's lifeboats had fallen into disrepair, possibly through lack of finance for their upkeep. The Redcar boat obviously fared better and there is reference to her being repaired in the *Visitors Guide to Redcar* (1848) by John Richard Walbran. As he only estimates the year as 1824 it is possible that it could have been earlier and that the repairs followed the incident recorded by William Ward Jackson.

'About 1824, "some repairs being requisite", the cork was removed and the more recent invention and application of a series of air boxes was made; forming, as it were, a seat of eighteen inches in width around the boat. These air boxes were made of copper, and are protected by a casement of oak wainscot. The alteration, though viewed at first by the fishermen with mistrust, has, however, proved of great benefit; and since the year 1820, upwards of one hundred and fifty lives have been saved. The boat has been greatly admired by nautical men for its elegance of form; and it is generally considered to be a very good one: indeed the men who trust their lives to it, have great confidence in its capabilities.' At some time eight drain tubes were fitted in the bottom of the boat so that it could free itself of any water taken on board. It is possible that they were installed at the same time as the other alterations were made.

24th October (1822). The brig *St Martins Planter*, in ballast, was wrecked on the North Gare. Her crew of nineteen were saved by Redcar lifeboat. The wind was south-east and stormy. Another account gives the name as *St Martins*, and that she was from Miramichi laden with timber.

1823

29th January. A boat from Redcar, returning from Seaton to Coatham, was overtaken off Coatham by a storm from the south west and rain. The crew of seven were saved by Redcar lifeboat.

1st February. Storm from the east-north-east. The brig *Friends Adventure*, of Stockton, captain Burnicle, bound light (without cargo) for Stockton, stranded on the North Gare, but was later got off. The brig *Beucephalus*, of Shields, in ballast, was wrecked on the South Gare and the crew were saved by Redcar lifeboat.

4th February. The brig *Mercury*, of South Shields, laden with coal, was wrecked on Marske sands. One of the crew was drowned and eleven saved by Redcar lifeboat.

The *Yorkshire Weekly Post* for the 13th October 1900 carried an article that told of how farmer J Beardshaw, of Tofts Farm, had heard signals of distress and raced to Redcar (three miles) to get the lifeboat. He was later given an inscribed cup for his action.

The brig was owned by John Eden and had previously been driven off course as far as Scotland by the storm. The hull was sold for £142 and the name of the captain was given as Laden.

Volume two of *Baines Yorkshire* was published this year and commented that, 'the coast of Redcar is very rocky, and the navigation dangerous, but an excellent nautical chart, by (Palliser) Thompson (a Redcar Pilot) has lately been published, which has greatly diminished the number of shipwrecks, and the Life-Boat, established here in 1802, which is very spacious and complete, renders these casualties less fatal when they do occur.'

1824

In March the 'Royal National Institution for the Preservation of Life from Shipwreck' was founded. The title was changed in 1854 to the 'Royal National Life-boat Institution, Founded in 1824 for the Preservation of Life from

Shipwreck'. It was generally contracted to the RNLI and is how the institution has since been known and respected throughout the world. For the sake of continuity and ease of identification the abbreviation RNLI is used throughout, whether before or after 1854.

Seven Redcar fishermen were drowned when their cobles were overtaken by a sudden gale on the 22nd December. The lifeboat was not brought into use and the lack of action prompted a letter of criticism from an anonymous correspondent:

'To the editor of the Newcastle Chronicle.

Sir,

The gale of the 22nd inst. has been more disastrous to the fishermen of this place, than any remembered by the oldest inhabitant. The wind, which in the early part of the morning was from the east, suddenly changed to the south and west; and, induced by the then tranquil state of the weather, the fishers ventured off. About noon the wind came round in an instant from the north east blowing with great violence, and in a very short time it increased to a dreadful gale, bringing with it a most tremendous heavy sea; great apprehensions were now entertained for the safety of the fishermen, who were seen approaching.

Had the Life-Boat, at this critical juncture, been got out, in all human probability, the lamentable catastrophe of that day would have been avoided; but from an unaccountable oversight that was not done. It is to be hoped that the fatal effects of this day will be a warning to the inhabitants at large, never to spare any exertions that may conduce to the preservation of their fellow-creatures, and particularly so, when they have at their immediate command, so fine a boat as that at Redcar, which has on so many trying occasions, manifested its capability of combating the most furious waves.

But to return to this eventful day, the cobles continued to approach the shore, and, in attempting to land, several were filled by the waves, then upset, several of the crews were washed out, and seven met a watery grave in the sight, and almost within the hail of their dearest relatives.

The scene at this moment was most appalling - the agonizing shrieks of the women, the heart-rending screams of the children, and the general consternation and distress of those who lined the beach, formed a picture of misery and horror, of which words can give but a faint outline.

The names of the seven poor fellows who thus perished are, George Robinson and his two sons, Christopher and Thomas; Thomas Hall and his two sons, Richard and George; and William Grey, senior, who was washed out with his two companions, they were saved by another coble, but he sank to rise no more. Several of the other fishermen had narrow escapes, and were picked up by the praise-worthy exertions of William Pott's coble, who put off, at eminent hazard, to their assistance.

A subscription has been entered into for the relief of the widows and children of the unfortunate sufferers, and it is hoped the benevolent public will commiserate their lamentable situation.

X.X.

Redcar, December 23rd, 1824.'

A letter in the *Newcastle Chronicle* of the 15th January 1825.

'Sir,

We, the undersigned inhabitants, mariners, and fishermen, of Redcar, having read in your paper, a letter dated Redcar, the 23rd day of December, 1824, reflecting upon the whole of the inhabitants, in not getting the life-boat out upon that fatal day when so many of our unfortunate townsmen found a watery grave, we therefore beg leave to state, that from the time of the gale commencing until the dreadful catastrophe happened, there was not the least possibility of the life-boat rendering any assistance to the unfortunate sufferers, owing to the shortness of time from the commencement of the gale to the end, which, in the whole, did not exceed a single hour.

What the writer can mean by casting such foul aspersions upon a whole town, is best known to himself. But we, for our parts, are firmly convinced, that no exertions were left that could be of any avail to the unfortunate sufferers. Many of us had our dearest relatives then struggling with the angry deep; can human nature think that we would not avail ourselves of every effort to render them assistance?

The Redcar life-boat has always done her duty in preserving the lives of our fellow-creatures in distress; and confident are we that the Redcar men will never flinch from their duty. Many of the undersigned are those who escaped upon that fatal day; and they are fully convinced, from the time they broke from their lines until they reached the shore, that it was utterly impossible for the life-boat to render them the least assistance.

Inhabitants: Christopher Moore, John Wilson, Joseph Newton, M. McNaughtan, Thomas Bell, Thomas Carleton, Jeffrey Smith, John Clough, James Carter, Joseph Dove junior, Robert Coulson, John Spurr, John Watkin, Gavin Brown, John Harrison.

Mariners: Ralph Carter, Robert Sheildon, George Atkinson, H.Henderson, Robert Burnicle, John Dixon, William Darnton, John Walton, Thomas Thompson junior.

Fishermen: Thomas Burnicle, T.Thompson, Jas. Carter junior, John Carter, James Fleck, William Potts, John Sheildon, William Upton, M Burnicle, Isaac Marshall, John Picknett, Richard Picknett, Henry Guy, John Thompson.

Redcar, January 10th, 1825.'

Letter in the *Newcastle Chronicle*, the 29th January 1825.

'Sir

On looking over your paper of the 15th inst. I saw with surprise a kind of protest from Redcar, signed by a few individuals, and containing unhandsome allusions to my letter, which appeared in the Chronicle of the 1st inst. What expression in my narrative of the occurrence of 22nd December could so dreadfully lacerate the feelings of these personages, and conjure up the protest, I know not; but I know that that narrative contained nothing but facts, and my comment on those facts was milder than they merited. Neither can I discover what part of my letter the protest invalidates, unless bare-faced assertions are allowed to pass for facts.

The falsehood of the assertion that the gale "did not exceed a single hour" must be known to all your readers in the North, and requires no further observation. Unfortunately for themselves, the protesters admit the truth of my former statement, that the life-boat was not even attempted to be got out, although, by their own account a whole hour elapsed. What were the exertions made during all that time? They say none were omitted, yet they do not specify any that were made.

Was even the drum sent round, as is usual when distress on the coast occurs, to alarm the inhabitants? It is true the sand, which had been suffered to accumulate against the boat-house door, was removed; and if I mistake not some of the protesters assisted at the work. Why, if they thought the boat could not render the sufferers any assistance, were they thus employed?

To those unacquainted with the place, it may be necessary to state that the boat-house was immediately opposite to the scene of action, not more than three hundred yards from the water's edge, to which the boat might be run down in ten minutes, and had it been found impracticable to get her afloat, was there not a possibility of her being anchored, and the rising tide would in a very short time have enabled her crew to get their oars in action? Certainly the natives who signed the protest will allow that this might, aye, and ought to have been done - at least the experiment was easy to be tried, and then no blame could have been attached to them.

As this was not attempted, how they could dare to say "no exertions were left" untried, is beyond my comprehension. Manning the boat, was at first the excuse for her not being off (although the protest wisely says nothing of that); but that obstacle vanishes when we have before us the names of nine seamen at the protest; doubtless they were there, or they would hardly offer their signatures to witness an occurrence at which they were not actually present.

Six preventive boatmen were in the town at the time; had the boat then been at the water's edge, and for want of hands, can we suppose they would not have offered their services? Undoubtedly they would have gone in the boat. Here were then a sufficient number of men, by their own account, there was sufficient time, and yet the boat was not dragged out, and a protest is got up to censure the person who barely hinted at the neglect!!

It is painful for me to reflect on the conduct of any individuals; more painful, when these individuals have, on former occasions, displayed greater foresight and presence of mind than on this melancholy occasion. Far be it from me to accuse them of wilful neglect (the light in which the protest would wish mine of the 23rd December to be viewed, but to the impartial mind it conveys no such stigma); "human nature cannot think so"; neither do I, that it was a wilful omission; but I repeat what I before observed, "that it was an oversight", and such I trust will never again occur.

I considered it a duty I owed to myself and the public, to make the observations on a protest signed by so few of those who were present, and among these few might be found some who were not even in Redcar at the time, much less present at the dreadful occurrence!! - I now take my leave of this unfortunate affair, conscious it has occupied much of your space already; and, with thanks for your impartiality, subscribe myself yours respectfully, X.X.

Redcar, January 20th, 1825.'

The church of St. Germains, Marske. All except the tower was demolished in the 1950s. The churchyard is the last resting place of many who were closely associated with the Zetland. Memorials can still be seen for members of the Dundas family, Henry Walker Yeoman and the Robinsons, father and son, victims of the 1824 coble disaster. The gravestones of others, including the unfortunates from the Caledonia *(1808), have not survived the ravages of time. (From a postcard in a private collection.)*

It was unfortunate that the critic chose not to reveal his identity. He was undoubtedly moved deeply by the tragedy but may not have had a seafarer's knowledge to understand the situation fully. It is a fact that when returning from sea in bad weather the greatest danger is often in the last few minutes before the shore is reached. A safe landing may be barred by heavy breakers formed when a rough sea is forced into shallow water. On a flat beach they may extend seawards for some distance. A steep, breaking wave can upset even the most expertly handled boat and leave the occupants struggling for their lives in its foaming wake. In such a case, speed of assistance is essential or loss of life must surely follow. Even if a lifeboat can be got to the scene in time, the disaster may have occurred in water that on average was not of sufficient depth to float it from its carriage. This may well have been the case on that fateful day at Redcar.

In the churchyard of St Germains, Marske, there is a gravestone with the inscription 'In memory of George Robinson and his 2 sons Christopher and Thomas, who all departed this life December 22nd 1824, aged 57, 24, and 17 years respectively'.

1825

29th September. The brig *Fleece*, of Sunderland, Booth master, bound from Sunderland to London with coal was wrecked on Redcar rocks. Crew of ten saved by Redcar lifeboat.

6th October. The brig *Richard and Ann*, of Sunderland, Joseph Dixon master, from North Shields to London with coal was stranded on Redcar rocks and got off next tide. Crew saved by Redcar lifeboat.

11th November. Schooner *Courieren*, of Stockholm, Westerberg master, from Gottenburg to Leith with deals and iron was wrecked on the South Gare. The crew of seven were saved by Redcar lifeboat and the cargo was saved.

17th November. The brig *Brittania*, of London, Taylor master, from Newcastle to London with coal was wrecked on Redcar rocks. Crew of nine saved by Redcar lifeboat.

1826

6th September. The Whitby whaling ship *Esk* was wrecked near Marske and 23 of the crew of 27 were lost.

Whitby Repository and Monthly Miscellany, Vol 2, number 14:

'Dreadful Shipwreck

It is our painful duty to have to record this month, the melancholy and unexampled occurrence of the loss of two Greenland Ships, the *Lively* and *Esk*, belonging to the port of Whitby. The *Lively* is reported to have been lost,with all hands, among what is called the "west ice", on the 19th of April last. This distressing account was made public at Whitby, on Saturday, the 2nd of September, by which the inhabitants of the town and neighbourhood were overwhelmed with the greatest consternation and anxiety. There are some persons half inclined to entertain a hope that she may possibly make her appearance, or at least that a part of her crew may have been saved; yet, it must be admitted, that there is every reason to fear the melancholy report will prove too true.

Great, however, as was the distress occasioned by the report of the loss of the *Lively*, that distress was increased in a tenfold degree, on the following Thursday, Sept. 7th, by the melancholy intelligence which reached here about 12 o'clock, that the *Esk*, of Whitby, Capt. Dunbar, which had been expected daily for more than a week, had come on shore during the tremendous gale, about 11 o'clock the preceding night, not far from Redcar, on the dreadful rocks adjoining to Marsk.

The ill-fated vessel, it was stated, kept beating against the rocks until a little after five o'clock in the morning, when she parted completely in two, and the crew, consisting of twenty-seven persons, were instantly precipitated into the foaming deep.

It was added, that twenty three of them had found a watery grave! that the Captain and three of the sailors had washed on shore; that the latter were fast recovering, but that the Captain, on arriving within a few yards of the shore, was so severely struck by a log of timber, which had floated from the wreck, that on being taken up on the beach, life was extinct.

The following additional particulars relative to the above mournful catastrophe, have been communicated to us by one of the survivors -

The *Esk* went into Shetland, on her passage home, about one o'clock in the morning of Sunday, the 27th of August, and left, for Whitby, between seven and eight o'clock in the evening of the same day, with the wind from the NW. Had very shy winds all that week:- the following Sunday were off Aberdeen, with wind very changeable, but in general from the land; for which reason we kept inshore the full tide, and then ratched off to carry the tide outside two and a half hours longer.'

(When off the Tyne the second mate, John Skinner, had left in the pilot coble after an argument with captain Dunbar. The incident probably saved his life.)

'Thus, by endeavouring to make all flood tide and no ebb, (to save the springs) were caught , close in, with the heavy gale from the NE. on Wednesday, the 6th of Sept. About four o'clock in the afternoon, sent royal yards down: eight o'clock, took two reefs in fore and main-top-sails,and one in mizen-top-sail: half after nine, or thereabout, the tack of main-sail gave way; and whilst hauling the main-sail up, the main-top-sail split. - All hands on deck.

Soon after this it began to blow so violently, with a tremendous sea, that the vessel became quite unmanageable: the master ordered the top-sail be stowed; the ship then warred down before the wind and sea: shortly afterwards fell in with broken water. About a quarter after eleven o'clock, the vessel struck upon Marsk rocks - dead low water: with beating so much she soon knocked a hole into her bottom. About twelve o'clock, by order of the master, the main and mizzenmasts were cut away to prevent the vessel from turning over - her beam towards the sea.

Shortly after the masts were cut away, fifteen guns were fired, one blue light flashed, and a lantern hoisted on the top of the cabin funnel; the lantern was washed down as fast as it was put up:- after beating for some time, the vessel slewed round with her stern to the shore; the cabin windows were then filled with lights, none knowing where they were. All hands now went below and prayed. After this they fastened her middle deck down, to prevent the casks from blowing the vessel up, at the same time hoping that it would assist in floating them to the shore.

Between twelve and one o'clock, the whole crew again fled to the throne of grace, and continued in prayer until the decks began to blow up by the making of the flood tide. Scarcely had all hands got upon deck, before she was up to her deck beams with water: one man, who had a broken leg, was hauled up on deck, and put on the larboard quarter, abreast the companion. Again all hands engaged in prayer.

The sea now made so very fast, that the whole crew were obliged to get as far aft as possible: the water began to force the casks up out of the hatchways, and by their flying about and among them in all directions, some whole and other in pieces, they expected every moment to have been killed. This was about three o'clock in the morning (Thursday).

From this time, until a little after four o'clock, so boisterous was the sea, and the vessel in so dreadfully shattered a state, that the crew were forced to cling to each other, and to anything that came in their way.

In consequence of the vessel beating down upon her starboard side so much, it was soon driven in; and the sea having obtained a free course, twisted the ship in all directions.

A little after four o'clock most of the crew got into the quarter boat on the larboard side; three clung to the quarter athwart the ship's davit. The main-mast, by raging about, worked the rigging off the mast head; and all being entirely gone from the mast, by its washing upon the crew it threatened them with instant death. A little before five o'clock, some of the men thought they discovered a Life-Boat coming towards them, others thought it was only a part of the wreck washing about: they instantly began to shout as loud as they could, and to wave their hands, hoping that what they saw might possibly prove the former.

The fore-mast, the fore-top-sail, and the fore-sail still remaining, the mate and one man ventured forward, and got into the fore rigging, (her bow being to the eastward) the master at the same time standing aft, without his hat, holding himself by the rail; in a few minutes, being about five o'clock, the vessel began to separate in the middle; in a quarter of an hour after, her fore-mast and bow fell on the starboard side, and her quarter towards port, with the remainder of the crew upon it. Thus all hands, nearly at the same moment of time, were plunged together into the foaming billows of the deep.

One of the three survivors was washed to the shore on a part of the stunsail boom; another on a part of the wreck; and the third on the above mentioned davit, he being one of the three who clung to it on board the ship. The last man had been lame for some time, in consequence of which, he had been obliged to walk with a crutch; and, what is very remarkable, the crutch washed to the shore, all the way close to the davit. As this man approached the shore, he got entangled in among the wreck, and would have been drowned, had it not been for two men who ran into the water, up to the waist, and rescued him.'

The three survivors were Matthew Boyes, William Leach (carpenter's mate), and William Pearson (the man with the injured leg). The logbook of the *Esk* washed up at almost the same time as the body of Captain Dunbar. It was thought that he had kept it with him to bring ashore.

A detailed account of the tragedy is given in a book, *The Loss of the Esk and the Lively* written by William Scoresby, a whaling ship captain of great repute. He had been given command of the *Esk* when she was a new ship in 1813. She had been damaged by ice in June 1816 and only the ingenuity and ceaseless perseverance of Scoresby had prevented her from sinking. Temporary repairs had been made with the aid of crews from other ships and she had safely made the voyage home to Whitby. John Dunbar had been one of Scoresby's officers on that near-fatal venture. They had served together as young men under William Scoresby senior, one of the best known whaling ship captains of his day. With guidance and encouragement from both Scoresby senior and junior, Dunbar's career progressed from able seaman until he was made captain of the *Esk* in 1817.

Of the day when the ship was lost, Scoresby wrote of how it had been tacked as close to the land as was prudent. The manoeuvre had been to gain advantage from the flood tide, which runs south at least two hours earlier inshore than it does further off. There had been an anxiety to reach Whitby during the spring tides, which were already past their greatest height.

The *Esk* was a big ship and needed the extra height of spring tides to get into Whitby harbour. To miss them would have meant a delay of several days until the next big tides. In the meantime the ship would have had to have anchored off the town. That would have pleased neither the owners, because of the extra expense incurred, nor the crew, who were in sight of their homes yet unable to reach them. A ship in an open anchorage was also in danger from sudden changes in the weather. Such were the dilemmas that drove captain Dunbar to make all speed. Scoresby continued:

'Very severe strictures, having appeared in the public papers, respecting the management of the life-boat, a few remarks on this subject may not be improper here. As soon as the signals of distress from the *Esk*, proclaimed, to the neighbouring inhabitants, the circumstances of her being on shore, it appears that they, along with the "Coast-guard", made every exertion for bringing the life-boat, kept at Redcar, into action. The boat was brought a considerable way along shore, and a grapnel or anchor laid out when the tide was low, for hauling her off by break of day.

But when the boat was to be manned, there were few hands that offered to embark in the laudable adventure. Lieutenant Lingard, of the "Coast-guard", with four men under his orders, jumped in, along with some of the fishermen; but the boat required ten hands more to be fully manned.

Finding themselves unable to make way against the heavy seas, with such a short complement of men, Lieutenant Lingard got on shore, with a view of endeavouring to prevail upon some more of the fishermen to embark; but though seconded in his efforts by a gentleman residing upon the spot, who himself had offered to embark if he could be of any assistance, he was not able to obtain any more help.

The boat, in consequence, proved quite inefficient for the service, though every exertion, it appears, was used by those who embarked in it; and after toiling, without making progress, until their strength was exhausted, they finally drifted on shore on the beach.

It is said, that a want of good feeling between the fishermen and the "Coast-guard", (a circumstance exceedingly probable) was the occasion of preventing them acting together. But were this the case - how lamentable to think that private animosities should not be submerged under a mutual interest for the safety of their perishing brethren!'

It was the opinion of Lt Lingard that 'had there been sufficient crew in the boat, the lives of the sufferers in the *Esk* might without doubt have been saved'.

Lieutenant Lingard (or Linguard) RN went on to lead a distinguished career in lifesaving. Whilst Chief Officer of Coastguard at Robin Hoods Bay he was awarded the gold medallion of the RNLI for his part in the rescue of the crew of the brig *Henry* in December 1828, and the crew of the *Esther* in April of the following year. He was drowned along with eleven others, including five coastguards, in a gallant attempt to rescue the crew of a brig driven ashore at Robin Hoods Bay by a violent gale on the 4th February 1843.

There was a dreadful inevitability about the loss of the *Esk*. If she had not been caught close inshore when the storm broke, or if the sails had not blown out at that crucial moment, there may have been a chance of survival. Even the time she was driven ashore was against her. Had it been two hours earlier she would have been left high and dry when the tide ebbed. Two hours later and she might have held together until after high water and given a greater chance of safety for her crew. The fate of twenty-three men seemed inescapable and was the greatest loss of life from a sailing ship to be wrecked on the Yorkshire coast.

1828

22nd February. Article from unknown newspaper.

'The utility of the Hartlepool and Redcar life-boats to the shipping interests of this country, and the cause of humanity in giving that aid to mariners in distress off the Yorkshire and Durham coast, has been so strongly exemplified during the tempestuous weather this winter, that we are glad to find a lively spirit manifested in support of these useful and highly necessary establishments.

The committee of underwriters at Lloyd's, with their accustomed spirit, have subscribed towards repairs £40, and also for rewarding men who have been out this winter, £21. Darlington Insurance Company, £20; also at the disposal of a committee, for further rewards when required, £20. The Tyne Club, Newcastle, £5. The Hope Club, Newcastle, £5. The Trinity House, ditto, £5. Several merchants of Stockton and Darlington, and ship owners of the Tyne, £17 4s 0d [£17.20]. And Thomas Backhouse, Esquire of West Lodge, near Darlington, a member of Lloyd's, has agreed to give a smaller boat, to be stationed near Tees Mouth, between the two already provided, the cost of which is estimated at about 100 guineas.

The boats are now got into a good state of repair, and in perfect readiness. Upwards of 100 guineas have been expended on that of Redcar within a few weeks. A balance remains in the Darlington Saving Bank, for cases of emergency. 164 lives have been saved by the Redcar boat alone.'

1829

14th August. The brig *Aurora*, of London, Oxley master, from Shields to London with coal, was wrecked on the North Gare. The crew of eight and the master and his wife were saved by Redcar lifeboat. Lt R E Pym took command of the lifeboat and was awarded the gold medallion of the RNLI for his bravery.

The story of that epic rescue is divided between two very different locations. The first part is at Hartlepool Maritime Museum. In a tin trunk, painted black and marked in white letters 'Royal National Lifeboat Institution', are the records of the long-closed Seaton Carew lifeboat station. Amongst the rolled documents is an account by William Proctor of attempts to rescue those on the *Aurora*. Almost 300 miles away, in Poole, Dorset, are the modern headquarters

A steersman's view of the Zetland. Around the inside and extending from beneath the thwarts to the deck is the 'casement of oak wainscot' that covers the copper buoyancy tanks installed in the 1820s. Four of the eight drain tubes are visible in the deck and the steering oars, or sweeps, are laid along the thwarts. The nearer of the drums, hanging on the wall on the right, is believed to have been the one used to summon a crew for the Zetland. The other drum summoned the crew of the Free Gardeners lifeboat. (Photograph by courtesy of Kirkleatham Old Hall Museum.)

of the RNLI. On the shelves in the library are the handwritten minute books of the early management committees. On pages brittle with age can be found the story of how the Redcar lifeboat went on to succeed where Seaton Carew had failed. When brought together, the two accounts record a rescue in the highest tradition of the lifeboat service.

An account By William Proctor of the loss of the *Aurora*:

'The *Aurora*, John Oxley master, with a cargo of coals, in making for the Tees on the 14th inst. with the wind at east-north-east, a strong gale and a very heavy sea, the tide about half ebb, took the ground at the lower part of the North Gare about 5 o'clock, struck very heavily and filled with water - in consequence the crew were in imminent danger. An attempt was immediately made from Seaton to rescue them, the lifeboat being taken to the Snook 2 miles by 5 horses and 3 men with the greatest alacrity, and put into deep water with the following persons belonging to Seaton; Wm Hood, Jas Bulmer, Wm Ellinor, Wm Wilson, Jas Lithgo (Sailor), Ths Waistell (Shoemaker), Ts Waistell Jnr, Ch Bell (Blacksmith), Rd Hays (Mason), Arth Burton (Cartwright), John Franklin (Hosteller), John Shutt (Shoemaker), and a Soldier.

After incessant labour at the oar for 3 hours or more, they could not come nearer the vessel than about 200 yards [180 metres] principally owing to a strong outset with a heavy fresh and a great sea, which prevented their entering the right channel, and were forced to return greatly exhausted.

A second attempt was made with the Hartlepool fishermen and Wm Hood with a flowing tide, when after great exertions they were obliged to return, very much owing to the sea coming in.

The *Aurora's* crew were rescued about 10 o'clock the same night by Redcar lifeboat.'

The lifeboat at Seaton Carew was of a similar design, although slightly smaller, to the one at Redcar.

Wm Proctor's account for the attempted rescue amounted to £7 17 6d (£7.87½). Payment was granted by the local committee (Thomas Walker, chairman) and a cheque was signed by T Randyll on the 19th August. William Hood received £1, the twelve men that had gone out on the first occasion each received ten shillings (50p), and seventeen shillings and sixpence (87½p) was paid to the owner of the five horses.

Copy of a letter sent to the RNLI:

'We the undersigned visitors and inhabitants of Redcar cannot refrain from testifying our feelings of admiration at the zealous activity and humane conduct of Lieut. Pym R.N. of the Coast Guard service through whose exertions the crew of the Aurora of London (ten in number) were chiefly indebted for the preservation of their lives being wrecked on the coast between the hours of 10 and 11 o'clock pm during the tremendous storm of the 14th inst.

Signed; George Wailes - Low Hall Leeds, Rev. George Marwood -Busby Hall, Micheal Thomas - Ladler M.P., Thos Mouson - Rector of Bedale, Revd. H Hildegard, R S Blanchard, Rev. H Mitten, Christopher Clarkson, H or F A Richmond, Wm Lauder, Thos Bird -surgeon, Jas Dove.'

Minutes of a meeting of the Central Committee of the RNLI held on the 16th September 1829 at 18 Austin Friars, London. (The headquarters of the RNLI at that time.) Present: T Wilson MP (chairman), G Palmer , and J Cazenove.

'Read a letter from Captain Sparshott of 27th August and letter enclosed from Capt Morgan Ret, Inspect. Commander Whitby of the 18th August and 6th September, stating the total loss of the Brig *Aurora*, coal laden, near the mouth of the Tees on the 14th August - and the persevering, courageous and intrepid conduct of Lieut. R.E.Pym Ret. and five Coast Guard men and twenty one other men, who set off in the Redcar life boat at 8 pm when the sea was so tremendously high and broken that it frequently made a complete breach over the boat, and the crew were in such danger of being washed overboard that they were obliged to lash each other to their seats.

They however continued their course and at 30 minutes past ten pm the lifeboat got alongside the vessel, when the wreck was found to have settled greatly in the sand and the sea breaking over her topmast heads; in this situation they continued a considerable time in imminent danger of being thrown upon her, which must have been destruction to all, but they succeeded in saving the entire crew and the master's wife - ten in number.

The Redcar Lifeboat Committee had given 10/- each to the 26 men, but in consequence of the nearly exhausted state of their funds, a larger sum could not be afforded them from that source, but this amount had not compensated them for the loss of shoes, hats etc. which were washed overboard.

Ordered: That in consequence of the very laudable and persevering conduct of Lieut Pym the "Gold Medallion" of the Institution be presented to him - and that an award of 10/- be made to each of the 26 men, in addition to the 10/- they have received from the Lifeboat Committee.'

Copy of a letter dated the 25th September from the RNLI to Lieut Richard Elsworthy Pym RN:

'Sir - I have the honour to acquaint you that I have transmitted to Cptn. Sparshott R.N. Deputy Controller of the Coast Guard, the Gold Medallion voted by the committee of the shipwreck institution to be presented to you, in consideration of your very intrepid and persevering conduct in saving the lives of the crew of the Aurora, Coal Brig, ten in number when that vessel was wrecked near the mouth of the Tees on the 14th Aug. I have to request the favour of you to acknowledge the receipt of the same. I have the honour to be sir your most obedient servant,

Thos Edwards, secretary.'

Richard Elsworthy Pym entered the Royal Navy on the 20th June 1809 as a first class volunteer on board the 74 gun *Bellona*. He went on to serve on at least eleven ships in a career that took him from home waters to those of the Mediterranean and the West Indies. In 1815 he was promoted to lieutenant and on the 28th October 1828 was appointed to the coastguard, in which service he continued until early 1837.

In 1848 he was given command of the six gun schooner *Spider* based in Brazilian waters. He returned in 1847 and was placed on the reserved half-pay list with the rank of commander in 1858. A lieutenant's naval pension was granted in 1866. Commander Richard Elsworthy Pym died about 1877.

There is evidence that an urgent request was received by the RNLI in August 1829 for a lifeboat that was smaller and lighter than the one at Redcar. It may have been that some difficulty was experienced in transporting the latter vessel to the scene where the *Aurora* was wrecked.

In September a lifeboat was supposed to have been despatched for Tod Point at the mouth of the Tees and a little over a mile from Redcar. The boat was to the design of George Palmer (a member of the central committee of the RNLI) and had been built by Harton of Limehouse. It pulled six oars and approximate dimensions were given as length 26 feet (8m), beam 6 feet (1.8m). Records have yet to be discovered of its success or otherwise and there may be some doubt as to whether it arrived at all. The placing of a lifeboat between Redcar and the Tees was the subject of a letter dated 16th July 1831, from Robert Botcherby, of Darlington, to the Rev Raisbeck, of Stockton. It is significant that no mention is made of a lifeboat having been placed there previously by the RNLI.

'Dear sir, I omitted to name to you the great want there is of another lifeboat stationed at the Tees mouth on the Yorkshire side of the Bay. From the heavy expense of leading the Redcar boat to wrecks there abouts the funds are seldom found adequate to insure that attention to a vessel so promptly required in cases of emergency. Can you from your lifeboat fund do anything towards one now? Mr Vansitaart will give the ground for a house and I think from the Darlington fund and subscriptions I could raise about twenty pounds. As I understand from Mr King at Redcar you are much interested in promoting the funds for those boats presently on this part of the coast, he requested me to name it to you.

I am sir yours faithfully, Robert Botcherby.'

A subscription was entered upon to place a boat between Redcar and the Tees but nothing came of it. Presumably the money raised went towards the lifeboats already in existence.

1830-1839

1830

20th January. Two vessels were stranded on Redcar sands. They were the brig *Jane*, of Sunderland, Robert Ayre master, from London to Sunderland in ballast, and the schooner *Robin Hood*, of Harwich, Emmerson master, from Harwich to Sunderland in ballast. The crews of each, numbering 7 and 6 respectively, were saved by Redcar lifeboat. The brig *St Martins Planter*, laden with coal, was wrecked on the North Gare. Her crew of fourteen were saved by Redcar lifeboat. The wind on that day was from the north-east.

25th November. The Dutch galliot *Berhardina*, Veluin master, bound for Hull with a cargo of bark and bones, was wrecked on Saltburn beach.

Jackie Stonehouse was a member of the lifeboat crew that day and recalled how the galliot had driven into Saltburn Bay with the flood tide and fetched up on Dowesdale Scar. As there was no wind the crew dropped anchor. The sea had grown heavy and they took to the ship's boat and got ashore at Huntcliff. The lieutenant of coastguard ordered his men to launch the coastguard boat as he intended to make a prize of the deserted vessel. After the coastguards boarded her the sea grew even heavier and began to break on board.

Word was taken to Redcar and the drum was beaten for the lifeboat, which was taken along the sands. By then the seas were tremendous. The lifeboat crew waited for a 'smooth' (a calmer period between the breakers) and launched with little difficulty. When they reached the *Berhardina* they found the masts and rigging in a tangle alongside and the coastguards drowned. Three weeks later the body of the coastguard lieutenant was found at the Tees by the father of Jackie Stonehouse.

1834

9th (or 10th) December. The brig *Mowbray*, of Sunderland, captain Grainger, from Stockton to London with coal, was driven ashore between Redcar and

Coatham. The wind was north-west and strong. The crew of ten were rescued with great difficulty by Redcar lifeboat.

After the lifeboat had returned to the shore it was seen that two boys who had lashed themselves to the rigging had been left behind. By then the tide had receded sufficiently to give a better opportunity to reach the *Mowbray*. Although there was still danger the coxswain of the lifeboat, George Robinson, launched a small boat and, unaided, brought the boys to safety.

For his noble act a subscription was entered into at Stockton and in the following May a silver tankard was presented to him by Mr Richard Dickson on behalf of the subscribers.

1836

17th February, Ash Wednesday.

A tremendous gale from the north-east and a new moon combined to create an extraordinarily high tide. At Redcar it washed down a wall of the Swan Hotel yard and burst open the doors of the Primitive Methodist chapel. Other buildings close to the seafront were in danger and to save the lifeboat house the doors were opened and the tide allowed to rush through.

The Tees rose higher than had been known for forty years and much damage was done along its banks. Many ships were lost due to the gale and damage to buildings was extensive.

At Scarborough the lifeboat was turned end over end, and 10 of her crew of 14 were drowned.

On the 24th May the Rev Thomas Pym Williamson died aged sixty-four. He had been thirty-seven years incumbent of Guisborough parish and vicar of Kirkby Stephen in the county of Westmorland. In 1802 he and Lord Dundas had placed an order with Henry Greathead for the lifeboat at Redcar. His second son, William Leigh Williamson, who had latterly acted as curate to his father, died on 30th April aged twenty-five. Both were victims of a cholera epidemic.

On Christmas day, a Sunday, the brig *Caroline*, from Shields to Aalborg with coal, was wrecked off Redcar. The lifeboat was launched with a crew of twenty-two, one of whom, a pilot named William Guy, was washed overboard and drowned.

The following account appeared in the *British Seaman*:

'The Danish brig Caroline, of Aalborg, was observed driving fast to leeward, notwithstanding all her endeavours to beat off (the gale being from ENE the first quarter flood). She struck on Saltscar and the crew of nine took to the rigging. A heavy sea floated the vessel and she drove over the rocks. The men took to their boat - as the Redcar lifeboat was on its way to them, manned by the intrepid pilots and fishermen of that place. The crew of the Danish vessel had not quitted her five minutes before a sea broke over their little boat and swept away all but two.

The lifeboat held her gallant course among the breakers (notwithstanding she shipped three seas) and when the cry arose "she is alongside - they are saved" a heavy sea broke over both boats and they were lost for some time to the sight of the anxious spectators.

When the lifeboat was next seen she was far to leeward, driving fast ashore, her crew bruised and bleeding and the oars on one side all shivered. Nothing more was seen of the crew of the Danish vessel, and William Guy, one of the Redcar pilots, who was standing up to throw a line, was swept away, leaving a widow (Mary) and four young children.

Not a vestige of the Caroline is left. There is also a brig ashore three miles north of this place, another at Hartlepool, and a schooner was seen for a short time this morning whose loss is accounted a matter of certainty.'

Jackie Stonehouse was a member of the lifeboat crew on that day and his account of what happened was included in *The Book of the Lifeboat* (1894). He remembered how 'Old Nannie Potts' had watched the *Caroline* through a telescope from her cottage. The crew had been in a group in the rigging as if consulting. They put the ship's boat over the side and got in.

In the meantime the lifeboat was launched by West Scar and rowed off a little way. Slater Potts had one steering oar and George Robinson the other. A small boat was sighted with a man in it, his arms around a thwart, clinging on for life.

The lifeboat made towards it and got within 'a coble's long mast of it'. William Guy stood up in the bows with a boat-hook in his hands. Above the roar of the wind and sea he shouted to George Robinson and asked where he was to take hold of the man. Robinson instructed him to get the boat-hook into his clothes or anywhere he could.

The seas were 'mountains high' and at that moment a great wave bore down on them. The lifeboat was turned to face it but she was completely buried and carried a considerable distance shorewards.

William Guy was thrown overboard and Will Smith jumped up and threw the end of a coil of rope after him. When the wave had left the lifeboat in its wake the rope was hauled in but Guy was not on the end of it. He and the crew of the *Caroline* had been swept away to their deaths. The brig broke up on the Gare and was washed ashore in four pieces.

The body of William Guy was found six weeks later by a young girl as she walked on the shore at Sandy Wyke, just to the north of Staithes. Jackie Stonehouse had a sister, Margaret, who lived at Staithes and she recognised the face of the dead lifeboatman as he was carried up through the village. She sent word by horse post to Redcar and arrangements were made for the body to be returned. The burial took place in the churchyard of St Peters on 9th March

1837. Had it not been for the chance recognition by a former Redcar woman, Guy would have been buried in Hinderwell cemetery. Just another victim of the sea in a resting place unknown to his family.

Another account of the tragedy claims that Guy was identified by initials on his stockings and underclothing. It also claimed that he had been in the Primitive Methodist chapel when he was told there was a ship in distress. The congregation were singing a hymn by Charles Wesley *And Am I Only Born To Die*. Guy gave his watch to someone to keep safe for him and ran to take his place in the lifeboat.

Others said by Jackie Stonehouse to have been in the lifeboat crew that day were Tommy Boagey and Tommy Bilton; the latter was so badly injured that he was in bed for six months and was 'never the same man after'.

1838

On the 8th April the brig *Belsay Castle* was wrecked on the North Gare, and 6 of her crew of 9 were lost. The tragedy led to criticism of the Redcar lifeboat in the columns of four York newspapers. Accusations were made by an anonymous correspondent and an exchange of letters set two brothers in opposition to each other.

14th April, *York Herald*. From an anonymous correspondent.

'Stockton,- Fatal occurrence in the Tees. - On Sunday last a fatal occurrence happened at the entrance of the river Tees. The ship Belsay Castle, of Sunderland, Capt. Robson master, and other eight of the crew, struck on the South sand about 8am and continued till 2pm when she parted, and went literally to pieces, as appears from the wreck the sands are covered with. Six found a watery grave. Three were picked up by the Seaton life boat, two men and a boy, who were found floating on a piece of timber; the boy, however, died with cold and extreme fatigue.

Our correspondent says it is singular that the Redcar life boat, which is the most celebrated in the kingdom for safety, was on the present occasion, never taken out, and he adds,- base indeed is the man who will not aid his fellow creature in need, and hard it was to see the sufferers hoist their flag in distress and take to their rigging, and yet the celebrated Redcar boat that has done miracles, to be kept back. The only cause, he says, was that the boat has been newly painted, and must be shown to visitors for what money the spectators please to give. The boat could have been taken down into smooth water by horses in an hour and a half if the life boat house doors had been permitted to be opened.'

The following article appeared in the *York Chronicle* of the 11th April, and the *Yorkshire Gazette* of the 14th April. The information would seem to have been provided by Stephen Coulson of Redcar.

'Asylum Harbour at Redcar, - Shipwreck on the 7th ult. We recorded the total wreck of the Brig Resolution of Sunderland on the Redcar rocks. The recent gale of Sunday last, the 8th inst., has afforded fresh proofs of the want of this harbour. The Brig Belsay Castle of Sunderland was totally lost in attempting to enter the river Tees, and we are sorry to add that six of the crew perished, and three were taken from the wreck in a very exhausted state by the Seaton life boat. It is much lamented here that the Redcar life boat was not got out, the fishermen and many of the pilots being firmly of the opinion that the whole crew might have been saved thereby. The person holding the key of the life boat house however refused to open the door, from what cause has yet to be learned. The brave crew of the life boat, with their usual alacrity to save their fellow men, were all in readiness, but by the apathy of the individual alluded to were prevented from adding fresh laurels to the many they have already achieved.'

'Redcar, 16th April

To the editor of the York Chronicle.

Sirs. In your paper of last week there is a paragraph headed "Asylum Harbour, Redcar", in which some severe reflections are cast on the Master of the Redcar life boat, stating that he refused to open the door of the boathouse for the boat to be got out, and leaving your readers to infer that in consequence of such refusal the Master and five of the crew of the Belsay Castle were lost. We beg you will set the matter right by stating in your next paper the following facts, and then the public may judge what credit is due to your Asylum Harbour correspondent's statement.

It is unfortunately true that six of the crew of this vessel were drowned, but no blame can attach to the master and crew of the Redcar lifeboat. The facts are these :- The ship was first seen from Redcar about 9 o'clock on Sunday morning, the 8th Inst, on shore on the North Gare, about a mile and a half from Seaton Carew (where there is a lifeboat) and six miles from Redcar.

It was then low water, and at that time, and for two hours after the crew could have saved themselves in their own boat. So confident was the master that there was no danger, and that the vessel would drift over the sand with the tide into the Tees, that he even did not hoist a Signal of distress. But as the tide flowed up the crew began to feel the danger of their situation (the ship being a very old one) and then a signal of distress was hoisted - but too late for any assistance to be given them from Redcar; for with the flood tide and wind directly against her it would have been impossible for the Redcar Life boat to have rendered any assistance whatever. We the undersigned committee of management for the Redcar life boat, consider it our duty to say thus much to refute the base calumny attempted to be cast on a brave and worthy man - who has at all times - and at all risks - ever been the first to brave all danger when the lives of his fellow men have been at stake.

37

We trust Sir you will hereafter be a little cautious in giving to the public the statements of your Asylum harbour Correspondent in such a case as the above, for it is calculated to do much injury, and could not possibly be productive of any good, even had his statement been true.

Signed Alex Tod - Lieut Col residing at Kirkleatham, Thomas King - Kirkleatham, Joseph Wilkinson - Minister of Redcar, Robt. Coulson - Redcar Agent to Lloyds, Christ. Moore - Redcar.'

'23rd April, Redcar.

To the Editor of the York Chronicle.

Sirs- In reply to the attempted contradiction of my communication of the 11th, instant, I state it is a fact that the vessel was seen aground little after eight o'clock; and as respects the distance, if any of your readers will take the trouble to examine a chart of the Bay and River Tees, it will be found that the distance to the place in question is not more than four miles, and the distance from Seaton lifeboat house (which is laid down on the chart) is very near two miles.

By referring to the tide table it will be found that it was not low water before 9.36am at which time and for two hours afterwards the Redcar lifeboat could have got alongside without any difficulty.

As your "Asylum Harbour correspondent" did not presume to give any opinion of his own in the paragraph complained of, he will now endeavour to maintain his position by a plain statement of facts, which he defies the committee with any consistency to contradict. First it is a fact that the master of the lifeboat was importuned to open the doors of the lifeboat house by several of the fishermen and pilots, and it is also true that Mr Robt. Coulson, agent to Lloyds, and Mr Robt. Sheildon, pilot, rode down the sands together to within a short distance of the vessel, when they were both so satisfied of the dangerous situation she was in, that they rode back to Redcar with all possible haste, when the same Mr Robt. Coulson repeatedly urged the master to get the boat out - with what success has already been seen.

It is moreover stated "that the master of the Belsay Castle did not hoist a signal of distress till too late" - The Committee may be asked if it be usual to wait for more signals of distress before the lifeboat is got out - when a vessel is on the bar of the Tees and the sea breaking over her; - and whether, when the moment a vessel has been seen in so perilous a situation, it has not been always heretofore considered a sufficient signal of distress:- no sooner were they seen in such cases, than a drum (kept solely for that purpose) was beat through the town, at which sound a force was always mustered in a few minutes doubly able to man the boat.

Much to the credit of the Redcar pilots and fishermen, such is their eagerness to man the boat that many feel sorely disappointed at being left ashore after a full crew is obtained. It is also true that the Redcar lifeboat while Robt. Sheildon Snr. was master, has often been got out in the stormy dark nights of winter when a signal could not be seen, and even under the disadvantage of darkness and amid the pelting of the pitiless storm many crews have been saved from a watery grave.

Your correspondent has only now to add that three crews have been saved by the Redcar lifeboat on the same place as the Belsay Castle, Viz the crew of a Swedish vessel the Magdalene, consisting of fourteen; the crew of the St Martins Planter consisting of sixteen (or nineteen); and the crew of the Aurora, of nine and a female passenger.

My reason for heading my communication "Asylum Harbour at Redcar", was that I trusted that common sense would make it instantly apparent that had Redcar harbour been completed the master of the Belsay Castle would have run for that much wanted deep water refuge harbour, and not have perished with his crew on the dangerous sands at the mouth of the Tees.

I beg also to state that five other brigs and a schooner which were also running for the Tees for refuge were apparently deterred from doing so by the fate of the Belsay Castle. They brought up and rode out the gale between the Seaton Long Scar buoy and the Tees Bar buoy. It is the opinion of nautical men that had the wind on the 8th inst been a heavy gale, they, in all probability would have suffered the fate of the Belsay Castle.

With respect to the present master of the lifeboat, his individual gallantry is unquestionable, and has been repeatedly proved. My opinion is that he has relied too much in this instance on the timely exertions of the lifeboat on the opposite side of the bay, which had the advantage of being to windward of the wrecked vessel. I remain Sir,

> your Obdt. Servant,
> Stephen Coulson.

PS I beg your readers to observe that Mr Robt Coulson the Agent to Lloyds, was the only person present of the five who have ventured to contradict my statement, Lieut Col Tod and Mr King being at their homes at Kirkleatham, the Revd Joseph Wilkinson was at Upleatham and Mr Moore was absent from Redcar.

Stephen Coulson wishes it to be distinctly understood that he had nothing to do with the writing or sending of the paragraph, relating to the wreck of the Belsay Castle, which appeared in the York Herald (14th April), neither was he aware that any such article had been written or sent to the editor of that paper, before the Herald containing the same arrived at Redcar.'

A copy of the preceding letter, and the one that follows, was sent by Stephen Coulson to his brother Robert on Tuesday evening the 24th April.

'Redcar Mill.

Dear Brother, Notwithstanding the late untoward affairs, we are still the offspring of one mother and as such I am determined not to quarrel with thee, although thou certainly was reprehensible in signing a document which was sent forth to the public declaring that thy brother was a liar; yet I say notwithstanding this we are brothers! and I willingly attribute thy signing the same as a hasty act, done without mature consideration, and as such believe me when I say that I yet love thee as one brother ought to love another.

So much respect had I for thy counsel as a brother that I determined in my mind, long before thou left my house on Saturday night, that I would make no reply to the scurrilous contradiction of my communication - I have however been advised not to sit down with it, and this too by some friends who were able to judge of the matter, and I have no doubt but I shall be able to convince thee that I had no other course left, had I not done so I would have been stigmatized as a liar, when the finger of scorn would have been pointed at me wherever I went. In doing this, it is to say to thee, who knows the whole affair that truth will bear me out in all I have asserted.

In replying to the attempted contradiction of my first communication I have been obliged to make use of thy name, but I have done this in such a way as will prove to the public that thou did thy duty in the melancholy affair to the very uttermost - and whoever may henceforth be blamed for dereliction of duty thou cannot.

As my reply may prove rather caustic to some of the parties concerned, and as thou may be consulted in the matter, I think it prudent to give thee a copy of my reply that thou may be prepared to answer them as a man and a brother - let the conclusion of such reply I have given the master of the boat the full credit for his former gallantry and concluded it saying that in this instance, it was my opinion that he had relied too much on the timely exertions of the lifeboat at the opposite side of the bay. This must not only satisfy Geo. Robinson but also the whole of the Committee concerned, at least if they have any pretensions to the better feelings of gentlemen.

Not doubting but this untoward affair will be productive of much good not only as regards the duty of the Redcar boat but also those on the opposite side of the Bay. I remain Dear Brother,
        Thine truly,
        Steph. Coulson.'
'To the editor of the York Chronicle.
Sir. Particular references being made to me in Stephen Coulson's letter which appeared in your paper of last week, I consider it my duty to state the following particulars, I first saw the vessel ashore shortly after nine o'clock A.M.: I immediately went to Geo. Robinson to know if the life boat should be taken out when not only he, but many others of the pilots, and nearly the whole of the fishermen were together, and it was then the unanimous opinion of all present that the Redcar life boat could not be got down to the Tees in sufficient time of tide to get to the vessel. It was also said that if any assistance was needed, the Seaton life boat was just at hand.

The weather now having become thick, I rode down to the Tees to see what had become of the vessel, and was soon followed by Robt. Shieldon Jnr. We ascertained that the vessel had driven a considerable distance near the Tees and was in less danger. The crew could then have left her in their own boat, having both wind and tide in their favour.

After waiting a considerable time on the sand, we observed a signal of distress, and then returned to Redcar to report what we knew, but I never yet demanded the key, nor urged the master to get out the boat. I am Sir yours respectfully,

     signed Robt. Coulson

The above is a correct statement of the case as far as regards myself. Signed Geo. Robinson, Master of the boat. Redcar April 20th 1838.'

No further correspondence on the matter has been discovered.

It is significant that the address of Stephen Coulson was the Mill, Redcar. In the *York Herald* of the 16th June 1838, the mill was advertised as to be sold by auction at the Cock Inn, Guisborough, on the 19th. It was described as a newly-erected and excellent wind cornmill of seven floors. There was also a newly-erected granary and drying kiln, a large house with a coach house and stables, a walled garden, and three acres of rich grassland. The house had an uninterrupted sea view and 'from its contiguity to the fashionable bathing place of Redcar, commands respectable lodgers during the season'.

It is possible that Stephen Coulson had made himself unpopular with his accusations, as the mill was close to Zetland Square where many of the fishermen lived. In the census of 1841 he was recorded as an engineer, aged forty, living at Coatham with his wife, Jane, and their fifteen year old son, John. It would seem likely that father and son were responsible for the 'Journal of Shipwrecks' that has been of such value in piecing together the story of the first lifeboat at Redcar. To be the source of such a vital legacy must more than vindicate Stephen Coulson for his criticism of the *Belsay Castle* incident, whether it was warranted or not.

In 1848 Stephen was listed as being a lodging house keeper at Coatham. He must have died a relatively short time afterwards as the 1851 census recorded that the establishment was run by his widow. Their son, John, spent some time away from the area before he returned and became innkeeper of the Cleveland Hotel, Coatham. He apparently retained his interest in shipping as he was also the reporter for the *Shipping and Mercantile Gazette*.

Robert Coulson, the older brother with whom Stephen had had such a difference of opinion, was the miller at Coatham. He was also Lloyds agent and the enumerator of East and West Coatham for the 1841 census.

The Asylum Harbour referred to in the letters had been proposed as early as 1832 by W A Brooks CE. The intention had been to use the reefs of rock that extend seawards from Redcar as foundations for piers or breakwaters. It was estimated that £1 million would have been saved in construction costs and the harbour would have provided 510 acres of sheltered water for ships caught in bad weather. The harbour would have been known as Port William and the expense of the scheme would have been recouped by a toll on passing ships.

In March 1859 the Harbour of Refuge Commissioners chose Hartlepool in preference to Redcar. Although they considered that Redcar was ' ... in no way inferior ... possessing greater depth of water, and, in some respects, superior facilities for construction. But Redcar, a place without trade or great commercial interests, can contribute nothing to the expense of a harbour; whereas from Hartlepool, a flourishing port of daily increasing importance, extent, and wealth, large assistance is to be expected in return for the local advantages it will derive from its creation.'

It was possibly the loss of life from the *Belsay Castle* that prompted a public meeting to be held at Stockton Town Hall on the 18th October. The chairman was the Mayor of Stockton, Christopher Lodge, and the subject under discussion was 'the expediency of placing the lifeboats at Redcar, Seaton, and Hartlepool, on some certain and permanent establishment'.

Among the resolutions passed unanimously were the following:

'That a committee be formed of managers of shipping companies at Stockton, Middlesbrough, and Hartlepool, and other gentlemen of the area, with Ralph Ward Jackson as honorary secretary.

That a second lifeboat be provided for Hartlepool by voluntary contributions, or in such a way as the committee may judge most advisable.

That the expenses be forthwith paid to the Life-Boat crew at Seaton for saving the crew of the 'Belsay Castle', and that J Moyle (collector of customs) be authorised to draw same from the bank.

That a rate of threepence [approx $1^1/_2$p] for each vessel of 150 tons register and under, and sixpence [$2^1/_2$p] for each vessel above that register for each voyage, be collected at the Custom houses at Stockton, Hartlepool, and Middlesbrough, from the date hereof, for the support and maintenance of the Life-Boats at Redcar, Seaton, and Hartlepool.'

1839

On the 19th February Lawrence, 1st Earl of Zetland, died at the age of seventy-two. The title had been bestowed on him on the 2nd July the previous year, less than a week after the coronation of Queen Victoria. Prior to that he had been Baron Dundas of Aske, the title inherited from his father, Thomas, who had placed the order for the lifeboat at Redcar with Henry Greathead.

1840-1849

1840

7th April. The sloop *Jane*, of Whitby, captain Lennard, bound from Newcastle to Stockton with a cargo of railway chairs, stranded at Saltburn. The crew of two were saved by Redcar lifeboat. The wind was north-north-east.

10th May. The barque *Arcturus*, of Whitby, Edward Hough (or Haugh) master, was wrecked on Coatham sands. A whole gale was blowing from the north-east (or east). Jackie Stonehouse remembered that the barque had a Downs pilot on board and that there had been grumbling amongst the crew that they should be in a place of safety before dark. Confusion arose over the flag on the coastguard house at Coatham, the Tees was mistaken for Sunderland, and the barque got ashore.

The lifeboat was taken along the sands and launched to the rescue. Every minute spent alongside the wreck was dangerous and there was no time to save personal effects. When a seaman came on deck with a bundle wrapped in a blanket a cry of refusal went up from one of the lifeboat crew. It was quickly explained that the master had taken his wife on the voyage and that the bundle was their ten day old child. The lifeboat brought all nineteen on board to safety.

The *Arcturus* later broke up and her cargo of timber washed up on the north side of the Tees.

A letter from the Lloyds agent to Jno Holt Esq, banker of Whitby, has survived and is preserved in a private collection.

'Redcar, 10th May 1840.

Sir, I beg to acquaint you that your Barque "Arcturus" Haugh, from Sierra Leone, to Sunderland Laden with Oak ran ashore today about 9 o'clock AM on the Coatham sands near the Tees - Crew saved by the Redcar Lifeboat - she will be a Total Wreck, as her fore mast fell some time before the LifeBoat got to her - I am requested by the Captain to acquaint you of the circumstance - you will come, or send, for the meantime, any, and everything shall be done to save the property - in haste, post time,

I am Sir, Yours truly, Robt Coulson. Lloyds Agent.'

June. A coble belonging to Mr Robson of Redcar, whilst returning from the sea with fish, was overtaken by a storm and the crew of three were saved by Redcar lifeboat.

From *The Local Records of Stockton and the Neighbourhood* By Thomas Richmond.

'10th December. At a public meeting held at Stockton respecting the preservation of life and property at sea (the Earl of Zetland in the chair), it was resolved that "the Shipwreck and Lifeboat Societies now existing in this place be incorporated, and form one society, for the purpose of providing a competent number of Lifeboats, of rewarding their crews and other persons who may exert themselves in the saving of life, and of establishing such stations for rockets and Capt Manby's apparatus, as may be deemed expedient, and supplying all other means which may be recommended for preserving lives and property in cases of accident by sea, and that such society be denominated The Tees Bay Lifeboat and Shipwreck Society.'

1841

12th January. Wind from the east. The sloop *George*, of Sunderland, from Hull to Sunderland with a cargo of iron, was wrecked near the entrance to the Tees. Six passengers had been transferred to a Scottish oyster boat when the sloop had been off Hartlepool Heugh.

As it was high water the lifeboat from Redcar was prevented from being taken along the sands. Instead it was taken to the scene by road. Gateposts were pulled up to clear a path but when the lifeboat carriage was taken onto the soft sand opposite the wreck the solid wooden wheels sank in up to their axles. A team of nineteen horses were unable to move it. The three man crew were drowned, and their vessel broke into four parts.

31st July. Two lives were saved by Redcar lifeboat. The men were taken from a coble, Adamson master, returning to Redcar with fish. The wind was northerly.

14th November. The brig *Susannah*, 225 tons, captain Watson, bound for London with coal, was wrecked on Coatham sands. The loss was recorded in *A Visitor's Handbook to Redcar, Coatham, and Saltburn* by G M Tweddell, published in 1850 and revised in 1863.

'On Saturday, the thirteenth of November, 1841, it was a calm, lovely evening, when the "*Susannah*", a collier-brig, sailed from Middlesbro'; an unseaworthy vessel, with a crew of eleven souls. During the night a tremendous gale sprung up from the south-east, and the brig, which was a very old one, became unmanageable. On Sunday morning, at the time of divine service, she was seen opposite Coatham, dismasted and terribly distressed.

The life-boat was manned at once, and every effort possible was made to reach her; but in vain. She was driven onto a sandbank, near the Tees-mouth, and in the presence of hundreds of spectators, every living creature on board perished, save a dog, which swam ashore; and in a very short time the ill-fated vessel was broken into shivers, and scattered in fragments on the beach, like the demolished plaything of some mighty giant. The Rev James Holme, B.A., then vicar of Kirkleatham heard of the disaster on his way to his Coatham lecture, and preached on the subject to his congregation.'

The lifeboat got close enough for the crew to recognise one of the seamen as John Boagey, a native of Redcar. John and Stephen Coulson record that the brig had left Stockton with a crew of nine, and that the gale was from the north-east. The brig was the property of the Commercial Shipping Co. Stockton, and the hull was later sold for £6. Eleven other vessels went ashore at Hartlepool in the same gale, two of which went to pieces.

29th December. A coble from Redcar, Atkinson master, was overtaken by a storm and the crew of three saved by Redcar lifeboat.

1843

4th February. In the early hours a tremendous storm blew from the north-north-east and did much damage to buildings in the area.

The brig *Liberty*, of Sunderland, M Liddle master, from Lynn to Sunderland in ballast, was driven ashore at Saltburn. Jackie Stonehouse remembered that the lifeboat was taken along the sands, and that abreast of Marske church the waves ran up the beach in great sweeps. There were fears for the safety of the horse team when one wave swept the lifeboat right off its carriage. The carriage was left where it was and the lifeboat was got afloat. The crew considered that conditions were too bad to get anywhere near the wreck and instead they made for Saltburn beck.

It was dark and a number of people were standing on the Huntcliff side of the beck. They saw the lifeboat turned sharp round for the shore and at the same time heard a shout from the crew of the brig. No more was heard and it was thought that the five on board perished soon afterwards.

One man had got into the ship's boat but the mooring line parted before his shipmates could join him. The boat washed ashore and the fortunate survivor had been taken away to be cared for before the lifeboat arrived.

27th February. Two cobles were overtaken by a sudden storm from the north whilst returning to Redcar with fish. Their crews, six in total, were saved by Redcar lifeboat.

13th (or 15th) March. Two cobles were overtaken by a sudden storm. Their crews, six in total, were saved by Redcar lifeboat.

17th October. During a sudden gale from the north-east a Prussian schooner, in ballast, passed over Redcar rocks and bore away for the Tees or Hartlepool. The lifeboat was got out but was not required.

18th December. Four cobles returning to Redcar with fish were unable to reach the shore. Their crews, twelve in total, were saved by Redcar lifeboat. There was no wind but a heavy sea.

1845

21st (or 22nd) December. A storm from the north-north-east. The schooner *Commerce*, of Stockton, Lister master, from Stockton to Dundee with coal, was wrecked on Coatham sands whilst making for the Tees. Her crew of six were drowned. She had left the Tees earlier and was believed to have put back because of the gale.

One account states that the *Commerce* was blown along so quickly that although the Redcar lifeboat was launched she was unable to catch up with her. The body of the mate washed ashore at Redcar the next day 'terribly mangled by the rocks'.

1847

The Hartlepool Lifeboat Association was formed and took responsibility for the lifeboats at that port previously maintained by the Tees Bay Lifeboat and Shipwreck Society. The latter body were still responsible for the Seaton Carew lifeboat on the north side of the Tees, the Greathead built boat at Redcar, and a similar boat, built by Gale of Whitby, and reputedly stationed at Tod Point between Redcar and the entrance to the Tees.

23rd November. Wind strong from the south-east (or south-west). The schooner *Samuel*, of Selby, eighty-two tons, Moat master, from London to Middlesbrough with iron (or in ballast), was wrecked on Redcar rocks. Her crew of six were saved by Redcar lifeboat. The estimated value of the vessel was £400. Four other vessels were stranded on the rocks on the same day and were later got off.

1849

A lifeboat was placed at Saltburn, which at that time was little more than a cluster of houses by the Ship Inn. The community was too small to muster a full crew and fishermen travelled from Redcar on a flat cart to make up the numbers. Presumably it was quicker to transport a crew the four or five miles to a lifeboat kept at Saltburn than to take the one from Redcar.

30th September. A severe gale from the north-east. The brig *Johanna*, of Dantzic, 227 tons, Witt master, from Sunderland to Dantzic with coal, was wrecked at Redcar. Her crew of ten were saved with difficulty by Redcar lifeboat. The value of the vessel was estimated at £1,500 and her cargo at £110.

The brig *Frankfurt*, of and from Ipswich to Shields, in ballast, stranded at Redcar. She was valued at £465 and sold as a wreck for £135.

The schooner *John*, of Saltcoats, from Riga to Hull with linseed, was lost off Redcar and her crew of five drowned. She was valued at £400.

The brig *Albion*, of Newcastle, 224 tons, Brotherton master, from Newcastle to London with general cargo, was wrecked on the South Gare and her crew of ten drowned. The vessel was valued at £1,600 and her cargo at £2,000.

As many as sixteen vessels were driven ashore between Hartlepool and Shields.

1850-1859

1850

30th September. The schooner *Albert*, of Feecamp, sixty tons, Vanneur master, from Middlesbrough to Feecamp with coal, was wrecked near Saltburn. One man, possibly the master, was drowned and six were saved by Redcar lifeboat. The value of the vessel was estimated at £500 and the cargo at £25.

1851

Mention is made of the lifeboat at Redcar in a report prepared for Algernon, 4th Duke of Northumberland, who took office as president of the RNLI in 1851.

The report lists the lifeboats, rocket apparatus, and mortars situated around the coast of the United Kingdom. It was noted that a mortar was much needed at Redcar and that the lifeboat was in fair repair and credited with having saved 200 lives.

1852

From Volume II of *The Life-Boat*, the journal of the RNLI.

29th October. 'Brig *Louisa*, of Riga, wrecked on North Gare near Seaton during a strong gale of wind from ESE. Crew of 10 saved by steam tug *Contractor* and the Redcar lifeboat. Reward of silver medal and £2.0.0 to Christopher Day, master of tug, and £1.0.0 to his 2 men. Crew of lifeboat rewarded by local association.'

The journal kept by John and Stephen Coulson gives the name of the brig as *Louise*, and that she was of Stettin, bound from Riga to Stockton with timber. The weather is described as a great storm from the east-north-east and the tide half-flood. Three of those saved are credited to the Redcar lifeboat and seven to C Day. A great many other vessels were wrecked along the coast with considerable loss of life.

In 1852 a new type of lifeboat carriage was built at the Royal Arsenal, Woolwich, under the supervision of Col Colquhoun of the Royal Artillery. It was the result of a request from the Committee of Management of the RNLI to the Master General and Board of Ordnance and was built at no charge to the RNLI.

The new transporter had four wheels, two of them in the form of a detachable fore-carriage. It was sent to Cullercoats, Northumberland, for trials and although found to be heavy three more were ordered for north country stations. In the minutes of a committee of management meeting of the RNLI, held in November 1853, it is recorded that drawings of the carriage and limber were sent to Redcar. No reference has yet been found as to whether the drawings were acted upon but the lifeboat had at least two different carriages during its career.

1854

15th November. The brig *Jane Erskine*, of Belfast, 232 tons, Park master, from Antwerp to Newcastle in ballast, was wrecked to the east of Redcar.

An account of what happened was given in *The Book of The Lifeboat* (1894) by Willie Dobson, then aged seventy-four and referred to as 'Master of the Old Lifeboat'.

The wind had been south-south-east and strong and the brig had stranded on Lye Dams scar before daylight. Most of the fishermen had gone off in their cobles to assist in an attempt to refloat her. Dobson had waited in a coble nearby with Jim Thompson and Charlie Cole. The sea had begun to grow (get rougher) and they were told to go ashore and wait until the tide had flowed. Dobson had just got home to a welcome pot of tea when a flag of distress was shown from the brig. The lifeboat was got out and some argument ensued as to whether to launch to windward of the brig or from Water Race, which was to leeward.

Robert Sheildon the regular lifeboat coxswain was not present and in his absence George Robinson volunteered and insisted on a launch to windward which would favour the lifeboat. The brig lay on her broadside with her keel to the shore. Those on board clambered on to the exposed parts to avoid the seas that broke over her. They had scarcely been taken into the lifeboat when the brig lay right down and began to break up.

The lifeboat returned to shore with about fifty people on board. John and Stephen Coulson record in their journal that the brig had a crew of nine on board plus eighteen pilots and fishermen who had assisted in the salvage attempt. Another account gives the number of those on the brig as nine crew plus twenty-six fishermen, and that the lifeboat had a crew of seventeen. No matter what the exact figure was, it was a great tribute to the lifeboat that it carried so many to shore in safety.

During the following night (16th November) the schooner *Tyne*, of Ramsgate, sixty-six tons, Jarman master, from Ramsgate to Hartlepool in ballast, anchored near the rocks off Redcar. Her forestay gave way and she later lost both masts and was driven ashore and wrecked. Her crew of five were saved with great difficulty by Redcar lifeboat.

1855

30th October. A gale blew from the north-east with rain. The brig *Rebecca*, of Shields, 169 tons, Webster master, from Dordt to Shields in ballast, went ashore on Coatham sands. Her crew of seven were saved by Redcar lifeboat. The brig was got off on the 9th November.

1856

8th July. A sudden gale from the north-north-east upset the coble *Brothers*, Boagey master, whilst returning to Redcar with fish. Her crew were washed overboard. One was drowned and five were saved by Redcar lifeboat. Five other vessels were driven ashore between Skinnigrove and Staithes in the same gale.

1857

Between the 3rd and 5th January a great storm blew from the east-north-east. It was estimated that more than 130 seamen lost their lives on the north east coast and at least twenty-three ships were driven ashore or sunk between the Tees and Hartlepool.

On the 4th the brig *Ann*, of Torquay, 146 tons, Winsbarrow master, from Torquay to Hartlepool, stranded on Marske sands. Her crew of eight were saved by Redcar lifeboat. The brig *Jane*, of Sunderland, was wrecked at Saltburn, and the brig *Emulous*, of Whitby, stranded on the South Gare. Her master had his hip put out of joint and the mate was lamed. An unknown vessel foundered off Coatham and her crew, believed to have been eight in number, were drowned. On the following day the barque *Emma*, of North Shields, 260 tons, McKenzie master, from Shields to Villarica (?) with coal and coke, was wrecked on Redcar rocks. An account of the rescue of her crew and the subsequent award of a silver medal to the coxswain of the Redcar lifeboat appeared in *The Life-Boat*, the journal of the RNLI.

'On the 5th January, the barque *Emma*, of Shields, was driven on the Redcar rocks, near the river Tees, on the Yorkshire coast. The Redcar life-boat was at once manned and proceeded to the rescue of her crew. After twice getting alongside her, owing to the breaking of their heaving ropes, the crew had to return in an exhausted state, having only rescued the master, as the vessel's crew, for some unaccountable reason, refused to get into the boat.

After obtaining some rest and refreshment, the life-boat's crew once more put off and succeeded in saving the remainder of the vessel's crew of 8 persons. The life-boat was reported to have behaved remarkably well on the occasion: she is the oldest life-boat in the kingdom, having been built on Mr Greathead's plan in the year 1802.

This life-boat is not in connection with the National Lifeboat Institution, but belongs to the Tees Bay Life-Boat Association. The Institution, however, awarded its silver medal to the coxswain of the boat, Robert Shieldon, in testimony of his gallant conduct on this and previous occasions. The crew were locally rewarded.'

Sufficient money was raised by subscription to present Robert Shieldon with a gold watch for his part in the rescue. Great credit was also considered due to the young men of Redcar, aged between 17 and 21 years, who manned the lifeboat and two cobles. No information seems to have survived as to what part the cobles played in the rescue.

In the same gale the Seaton Carew lifeboat (which was thirty-four years old) was damaged in an attempt to rescue the crew of the brigantine *Jubilee*. She had previously been out to the *Empress*. Repair or replacement of the lifeboat may have proved too expensive to be met by local funds, for in February the Seaton Carew lifeboat station broke away from the Tees Bay Lifeboat and Shipwreck Society and joined with the RNLI.

Hartlepool had broken away ten years earlier when the Hartlepool Lifeboat Association had been formed. Stockton continued with financial support for the Tees Bay Lifeboat and Shipwreck Society which then had lifeboats on only the Yorkshire side of the Tees.

23rd March. The sloop *Margarethe*, of Carolinesiel (or Carolinesigh), fifty-four tons, Meenan master, from Carolinesiel to Hull with beans, was wrecked on Coatham sands. The wind was from the north-east and very stormy.

The master was washed overboard and drowned whilst the vessel was off Redcar. His two sons and the mate were saved by Redcar lifeboat and taken to the Lobster Inn, Coatham. The boys had suffered greatly from the cold and their ordeal and were 'wrapped in blankets, well rubbed with warm flannels, and hot bottles applied to restore animation and vitality, internal stimulants

The gravestone of young brothers Wilhelm August and Haye Meenen in Coatham churchyard. Despite being rescued by the Redcar lifeboat they failed to survive the cold and the shock of their ordeal. (Photograph by Jane Foreman.)

to rouse actions.' Sadly all efforts to revive them were unsuccessful. They were buried in Coatham churchyard and the inscription on their tombstone can still be read: 'Here rest the bodies of Wilhelm August Meenan, aged 14, and Haye Meenan, aged 11, who were shipwrecked in the Margarethe of Carolinesigh, Hanover, on Sunday March 22nd 1857.' The mate, after a short period of careful nursing, was able to return to his own country.

1858

On the 21st July the Tees Bay Lifeboat and Shipwreck Society applied to be taken over by the RNLI. At the next RNLI committee of management meeting, held on the 5th August, it was 'decided to bring into connection with the Institution the Tees Bay Lifeboat Association which had under its management lifeboats at Redcar, Saltburn, and Middlesbrough.' The transference of boats, stores, etc took place on the 6th September.

At an RNLI committee of management meeting held on the 7th October it was decided, on the recommendation of the inspector, that the lifeboathouse at Redcar would be rebuilt. The honorary architect of the RNLI, C H Cooke, provided drawings for the new building and the annual report of 1859 showed that the cost of erection had been £148 10s (£148.50).

1859

On the 14th February Redcar pilot George Robinson died at the age of sixty-three. He had also been coxswain of the lifeboat and his memory as such was held in esteem long after his death.

About 10pm on the 25th October a strong breeze began to blow accompanied by heavy rain. By midnight it was blowing a terrific gale and a heavy sea was running. On the following day the Redcar lifeboat was launched to the Hartlepool pilot coble *Isabella*, which was in great danger, and her crew of two were brought to safety. Expenses of the rescue to the RNLI were £13 7s (£13.35).

26th November. The Prussian brig *Fortuna* ran aground on Eastscar and her crew of eleven were saved by Redcar lifeboat. Expenses of the rescue to the RNLI were £22 15s (£22.77). The brig was later refloated.

4th December. The Redcar lifeboat saved the crew of nine from the galliot *Marianne*, which had run aground on the rocks during a strong gale from the south-south-west. Expenses of the rescue to the RNLI were £20. The *Marianne*, of Rotterdam, in ballast, had been on her way to Middlesbrough and was later refloated. Two other ships got on the rocks in the same day.

In the 1970s a poster was saved from being thrown away by Redcar lifeboatman John Puckrin. It had been printed by J Proctor, printer of Southgate, Hartlepool, and was dated 15th December 1859:

'NOTICE

The Fishermen and Pilots of Redcar have all agreed not to Man the Life-Boat, or any other Boat, if WILLIAM THWAITES, Auctioneer, is allowed to interfere when doing their Duty in Saving Life or Property.'

The Redcar census of 1861 recorded that William Thwaites, auctioneer, aged thirty-eight, lived at 156 High Street with his Scottish wife, Martha, and their four year old son. What he did or said that so offended the fishermen and pilots has not survived the passage of time.

1860-1869

1860

From *The Natural History of Redcar and Its Neighbourhood* by D Ferguson.

'The Redcar lifeboat with its gallant crew is ever ready to aid with most praiseworthy exertions, the too frequent scenes of distress on this dangerous coast; and from the admirable manner in which the boat behaves in tremendous seas, the boatmen are fully convinced of her superiority over any other boat on the coast.'

The elements mocked these words on the 28th May when a sudden storm blew from the east-north-east of sufficient violence to uproot trees. It was accompanied by heavy snow and great numbers of sheep in the area were killed by the severity of the conditions. Twenty-four ships were driven ashore between the Tees and Saltburn and the *Corra Linn*, of Stockton, was lost with all hands at the entrance to the river. The sea must have been exceptionally rough as the lifeboat was recorded as having been 'on duty but useless'.

1861

In January work began on a massive breakwater that would change forever the geography of Teesmouth. The intention was to create a much needed harbour of refuge and thereby reduce the loss of ships and lives that all too frequently accompanied storms along the coast.

The entrance to the Tees was flanked by two sandbanks known as the North and South Gares. (The *Webster New International Dictionary* of 1914 defines gare as a triangular piece, and also warns beware! take care!) At low water the depth on the bar was as little as 3 feet (91.5cm). The intention was to encourage the scour of the river and increase the depth of water on the bar, thus allowing ships to eventually be able to make safe entry at any state of the tide.

The lifeboat at Redcar had been used for a number of rescues on the north side of the river but that was no longer possible when work had commenced on the breakwater. The core of the construction was slag, an unwanted by-product of iron-making that would otherwise have been dumped far out to sea.

It was considered that the use of slag would reduce the cost of construction from an estimated £600,000 to a mere £100,000. The final nett cost was £219,074 12s 7d (£219,074.63). The work took twenty-seven years to complete and the breakwater extended 2½ miles (4½km) from its starting point at Tod Point. It was named South Gare after the sandbank on which it had been built. 5,000,000 tons of slag had been used and 18,000 tons of Portland cement. By 1881 the depth on the bar at low water was 19 feet (5.7m).

On the 9th February a gale blew from the east-north-east that was considered the worst in living memory. A great number of ships were lost and many seamen perished. At Whitby the lifeboat was capsized and 12 of her crew of 13 were drowned.

From volume V of *The Life-Boat*:

'Redcar. On 9th February the brig *Roman Empress* was driven ashore near Redcar in a very heavy gale and high surf. The Redcar lifeboat was launched and proceeded to her aid taking off her crew of 10 persons and landing them in safety. Expenses £16-1-6d [£16.07½].'

The *Roman Empress*, of North Shields, Driver master, was bound from North Shields to Naples with coal. She was later got off.

There were five other ships ashore in the Redcar area. The brig *Mary*, of Sunderland, was wrecked on Redcar sands. The barque *Koh-I-Noor*, of Sunderland, was wrecked on Bran sands at the entrance to the Tees. Her crew reached safety in the ships boat assisted by Jack Picknett and David Thomas of Redcar. One of the crew had a broken leg and Robert Jordison rode to Redcar for a cart to convey him to the Swan Hotel. The brig *Eustace*, of Sunderland, stranded on Redcar rocks but was later got off. The brig *Lady De Crespigny* (or *Lady De Cressigney*), of Colchester, was wrecked on Redcar rocks and her crew of nine drowned. The Dutch schooner *Appollos* was wrecked on Redcar rocks and her crew of six drowned.

The bodies of three sailors were washed up and buried in one grave in Redcar churchyard on the 15th February. Their names were not known but two were believed to be from the *Lady De Crespigny* and one from the *Appollos*.

1862

At a meeting of the committee of management of the RNLI on the 6th March was recorded 'the services of the Redcar lifeboat in going off in a heavy sea and bringing into Hartlepool the derelict schooner *Banff*, of Harwich, which was found abandoned off Redcar on 2nd February.' The lifeboat crew were paid by the owners of the derelict vessel.

The RNLI boathouse built in 1859. It housed the Zetland from then until 1864 when she was damaged during a rescue and condemned to be broken up. The boathouse provided shelter for seven Redcar lifeboats before it was demolished in 1972 to make way for the present lifeboat station. (Photograph by the author.)

A local account states that the schooner had driven in from the east and sank off 'East Rock'. 'When she laid down the sea covered her sails so that she never rose again, the crew were all drowned in sight of those on shore.' The cargo is given as either coal or linseed.

1863

On the 11th September the following entry was made in the logbook of Zetland School by the head teacher James Roscoe.

'Lifeboat out this morning. 25 boys entered school at 10 o'clock. Have determined to close the doors at half past nine in future. Gave notice to that effect.'

As there is no record of a shipwreck on that date it is probable that the lifeboat had been launched on one of the quarterly exercises held for the benefit of the district inspector of the RNLI.

1864

On the 12th February a severe gale blew and continued for several days. On the 16th two vessels were wrecked on Saltscar. The crew of one, a schooner laden with coal, were rescued by cobles, and the crew of the other, the brig *Brothers*, in ballast, by Redcar lifeboat.

The following account appeared in *The Life-Boat*:

'Feb. 17th. The Redcar life-boat put off and rescued the crew of 7 men from the brig *Brothers*, of South Shields, which was totally wrecked during a storm on Redcar Rocks. Expense of service £27.16s (£27.80p). (The Redcar life-boat is the oldest in the kingdom - having been built in the beginning of the present century - and in performing this service was so severely injured that the Local Committee decided to condemn her as unfit for further service.)'

On Wednesday 24th June 1931, the *North Eastern Daily Gazette* published an interview with former mariner and lifeboatman, Thomas Hood Picknett, who was then aged eighty-six. He recalled that the rescue from the *Brothers* had been his first time out in the lifeboat.

'A boat came ashore and fishermen went out in cobles and took off the entire crew: they had just cleared the wreck when another vessel hove in sight and deceived by the riding light in the rigging of the first vessel, she ran aground. After landing the first crew, the fishermen went off in the lifeboat and managed to get the second crew aboard. They had just cut away when a wash over the wreck lifted the lifeboat on to the rocks and broke her keel. There were 37 souls on board and fortunately she survived and clearing at the next run of waves, made the beach.'

In addition to the damage to the keel, a further inspection of the boat revealed evidence of dry rot.

A new lifeboat and carriage were allocated to Redcar and arrived on the 12th September. They had been transported free of charge by the Great Northern Railway Company. The boat was of the self-righting type and of a very different design to the old boat it replaced. The keel was straight and the beam narrower. A rudder and a distinct bow and stern rendered it less manoeuvrable. The old boat was the same shape at either end and steered by long oars, or sweeps. The arrangement allowed it to be rowed ahead or astern with equal ease. The cost of the new boat (£300) and its carriage had been the gift to the RNLI of John Crossley and Sons of Halifax. Appropriately the boat was named *Crossley*.

The old lifeboat was condemned to be broken up as was the standard

Thomas Hood Picknett portrayed by Redcar photographer W H Taylor.
Thomas Hood Picknett lived in accommodation over the Free Gardeners
lifeboat house for almost 60 years. As a youth of seventeen he went out with
the Zetland in February 1864 and helped to save the crew of the brig
Brothers. *It was his first rescue and the start of a distinguished association*
with lifeboats at Redcar. He knew well the tragedy that the sea can bring.
On the 9th January 1901 he was one of the crew of the coble Perseverence
when it capsized whilst trying to reach the stranded steam trawler Honoria.
He survived but two of his sons and a brother were drowned. (Photograph by
courtesy of Kirkleatham Old Hall Museum.)

procedure for lifeboats unfit for further service. Stories of how it was saved are many and contradictory. What is without doubt is the tremendous feeling of pride and affection that the local people held for it. Attempts at demolition were halted by cries of indignation from the crowd that had gathered: 'Hold a bit, she's as sound as 'ivver, and better than new 'uns!'.

Two fishermen were chosen as spokesmen and met with Captain John Ross Ward, chief inspector of the RNLI. Their plea for the boat to be spared was granted and mentioned in *The Life-boat* of the 1st October 1864:

'The old boat, now replaced, was the oldest life-boat in the United Kingdom, having been built in the year 1802. She was on the original Greathead, or North Country model. She had at different periods saved a very large number of lives, and her crew had unbounded confidence in her. Having been handed down from one generation to another amongst them, and never having met with any serious accident, they entertained a great affection for her; and although unfit to go again afloat, they have requested that they may be allowed to retain her as a reminiscence of the past.'

The morning after the attempt at destruction, Henry Walker Yeoman rode up on horseback to view the boat. He promised the fishermen that stood by it that he would speak to his brother-in-law, the Earl of Zetland, with regard to having repairs made. A local subscription was entered upon to which Redcar fishermen contributed half-a-crown (12$\frac{1}{2}$p) each. Lord Zetland and Henry Walker Yeoman assisted and sufficient money was raised for the old boat to be repaired at South Shields at a cost of about £100.

At the time of the controversy Lord Stratford de Redcliffe was staying with Lord Zetland at Upleatham Hall. He had been British Ambassador at Constantinople during the Crimean war - 'The great Elchi, at whose nod the Turks trembled'. Moved by the pride and affection that the old lifeboat had stirred he wrote a poem that was later set to music by Claribel and published by Messrs Boosey and Co.

The Old Lifeboat

The Lifeboat, oh! the Lifeboat, we all have known so long,
A refuge for the feeble, the glory of the strong;
Twice thirty years have vanished since first upon the wave
She housed the drowning sailor, and snatched him from the grave.

Let others deem her crazy, nor longer fit to breast
The surge that, madly driven, bears down with foaming crest;
But we, who oft have manned her, when death was on the prow,
We cannot bear to leave her, nor will we leave her now.

Our fathers, long before us, her worth in danger tried;
Their fathers, too, have steered her, amidst the boiling tide;
We love her, - 'tis no wonder, - we can but follow them;
Let heav'n, but never word of man - the dear old boat 'condemn'.

The voices of the rescued, - their numbers may be read, -
The tears of speechless feeling our wives and children shed, -
The memories of mercy in man's extremest need, -
All for the dear old Lifeboat, uniting, seem to plead.

The Power unseen that lashes to storm the briny pool,
And, when the blast is keenest, forbids our hearts to cool, -
The hand of earthly kindness, that gave our Boat its life,
That made it, bird-like, flutter o'er waves in deadly strife, -

And now that Kindred Spirit, who makes the poor His care,
Shall heed our fond remembrance, nor spurn the seaman's prayer:
Another craft, and brighter, may stem the raging gale; -
Thy plea of sixty winters, old friend! can never fail.

Thine age shall be respected, thy youth perchance restored,
And sires and sons together shall press thy heaving board:
No fear that storms be wanting: and, call it old or new,
We'll cheer the boat that's foremost to save a sinking crew.

1866

Strong support continued for the old lifeboat and the repairs that had been made gave her a new lease of life.

From volume VI of *The Life-Boat*:

'10th November. The brig *Whitburn*, of Stockton, struck Redcar rocks during the night in thick and hazy weather. The two lifeboats stationed in the locality put off to the rescue of the vessels crew. Redcar old lifeboat reached the wreck first and succeeded in rescuing the crew of 6.'

Expenses paid by the RNLI for their own boat, *Crossley*, £16 13s (£16.65). The brig, under the command of captain Euston, had been bound from London to Middlesbrough and became a total wreck.

Sixty-six years later the incident was recounted to a *Cleveland Standard* reporter by Thomas Hood Picknett on the occasion of his eighty-sixth birthday:

'It was on Saturday night, as I well remember. It was about 11 o'clock, and a nasty night, you understand, when I sees a ship a blazing of its lights for help.

Well I knows the men were at Tommy Hall's - he kept the Stockton Hotel then, and public houses didn't shut till 11 or 12 in those days. So I went over to Tommy Hall's and brought the men out, and we went to the boat. Our old boat, you understand. Well, we'd to bring it right from Beech Road down to the front here, but we got it launched and saved every man aboard that vessel. Then when we gets back there was the new boat [the *Crossley*] manned by a lot of landlubbers, just setting out. Mr Picknett chuckled as he thought of it'.

1867

The RNLI lifeboat *Crossley* failed to win the confidence of the fishermen and pilots of Redcar. Although she was longer than the old lifeboat there was less space for the crew. The restriction was caused by the large air boxes at bow and stern that helped to right the boat automatically if it was capsized. In an effort to resolve the situation the RNLI transferred the *Crossley* to Middlesbrough and sent a larger boat to Redcar.

Extract from *The Lifeboat* of the 1st January 1868:

'The Redcar life-boat men having refused to work their boat, as they considered it was not large enough, a larger and more roomy life-boat has been supplied to them in its place. It is a very fine boat, 36 feet (11m) long and 9½ feet (2.9m) wide, and pulls 10 oars, which are always double manned. It is provided with a transporting carriage. The expense of the new boat, carriage, and equipment, has been benevolently contributed by the people of Burton-on-Trent, through the kind exertions of M T Bass, Esq., M.P., A O Worthington, Esq., Mr J Nichols, and other gentlemen and ladies.

Before being taken to its station, the life-boat was sent to Burton, and exhibited there from the 12th to the 19th July last. On the latter day, being the occasion of the Horticultural Exhibition, an imposing demonstration took place with the boat. It was first paraded through the town and then presented to the Society by Mr Bass, in the presence of a large concourse of spectators. Mrs Abram Bass then named the boat, which was thereupon launched into the river Trent, and afterwards, with much difficulty, capsized, and the self-righting and other qualities shown, everything passing off in the most satisfactory manner. The London and North Western, Midland and North Eastern conveyed the boat free over their respective lines to its station via Burton.'

The new lifeboat did little to satisfy the fishermen and pilots and there were many who still preferred the old vessel.

1869

Mention is made of the old lifeboat in *Watering Places of Cleveland* by S Gordon: 'The veteran boat is still staunch and strong, and we have no doubt will, for years to come, find stout hearts and willing hands to man her on her noble errands to snatch human life from the jaws of death on the angry sea.'

At some time during the year the lifeboat at Saltburn, formerly of the Tees Bay Life-Boat and Shipwreck Society, was named *Appleyard* by the RNLI. In a log book of shipwrecks kept by Mr A Picknett he noted that the Tees Bay Lifeboat and Shipwreck Society had two lifeboats on the Yorkshire side of the river. They were the old boat at Moore Street, Redcar, and the *Princess Alice* at the Bank End, Coatham. The latter had been a prize in what would seem to have been a lifeboat race at Hartlepool and had been won by the fishermen of Redcar in the old lifeboat. They named their prize *Princess Alice* and it was later removed to Saltburn. Mr Picknett added with indignation: 'she was not given to the RNLI by Appleyard'.

In *A Visitors Guide to Redcar* (1848), J R Walbran gives a description of the old lifeboat and adds 'Another lifeboat of similar dimensions, and constructed on the same plan, was built about seven years ago by Gales of Whitby; and is kept in a small building near the mouth of the Tees, near the extreme point of land West of Redcar'. This would seem to be the same lifeboat referred to by Mr Picknett although the exact date when it was built has not been established.

Princess Alice, the second daughter of Queen Victoria, was born on the 25th April 1843. The date could be indicative of when the lifeboat came into the possession of the fishermen as it is probable that it was named in celebration of the royal birth.

From volume VIII of *The Lifeboat*:

'The lifeboat (*Burton-on-Trent*) performed a noble service on the 2nd December, 1869, in saving at great risk the crew, consisting of 3 men, of the sloop *Frances Mary*, of Inverkeithing, which vessel became a total wreck on the Redcar Rocks during a strong northerly wind and in a very heavy sea. The old Redcar lifeboat put off as well as the *Burton-on-Trent*, but after contending for some time with the heavy seas, the latter boat reached the scene of the wreck half an hour before the old boat. There was, however, not sufficient water where the vessel lay among the rocks to enable the lifeboat to get alongside her, and a portion of the crew of the boat then waded between the reefs to her, some of them being up to their necks in water, and eventually the poor shipwrecked men were got into the lifeboat and were safely landed.'

The sloop *Frances Mary*, captain Phillips, who was also the owner, had been bound from Dunkeld to London with potatoes. She later floated off and sank.

1870-1879

1870

Redcar and Saltburn-by-the-Sea Gazette, Friday 21st January:

'On Friday evening, the 14th inst, a supper was given to the crews of the three lifeboats, vis. - the old and new boats at Redcar and the National Institution boat at Saltburn, at the Globe Hotel. The cost of which was defrayed by a subscription headed by the Earl of Zetland. The intention was to draw together in a friendly intercourse the whole of those connected with the lifeboat service, whether on sea or on shore. More than one hundred invitations were issued, and upwards of eighty availed themselves of the invitation, and partook of the splendid entertainment provided by the host and hostess, Mr and Mrs Wren. A very pleasant evening was spent in talking over their various experiences and adventures, interspersed with singing and other social enjoyments, which were entered into thoroughly by all present, and great good feeling seems to have prevailed. There was only one drawback, vis., that the crew of the old lifeboat was not fully represented, which was much regretted, as it was hoped to have a full gathering of all the crews.'

During the year the RNLI introduced a colour coded system for oars in lifeboats. A pulling lifeboat was steered mainly by its oars as it seldom gathered sufficient speed for the rudder to be effective. As a lifeboat reared and plunged in rough seas the rudder spent much of its time out of the water. It was therefore only of real use when a boat was under sail. (Lifeboats of similar design to the old boat at Redcar had neither rudder nor sails.)

To make them turn under oars, the oarsmen on the outside of the turn continued to pull and those on the inside backed their oars. Their efforts were assisted by two long steering oars set over the stern of the boat and handled by the coxswain and second coxswain.

It was sometimes difficult for the oarsmen to differentiate between the orders for starboard and larboard (the old term for port). Shouted above the shriek of the gale the words could understandably be confused. It was for this reason that the RNLI adopted different colours for oars - blue for those on one side, white for those on the other, and red for the steering oars (called sweeps). A coxswain needed only to shout 'Pull on your blues!' or 'Back your whites!', or whatever combination was necessary.

1871

A lengthy account in the *Redcar and Saltburn-by-the-Sea Gazette* of the 6th October commented on 'the recent publication of the Wreck Register - the "black list" as it is often called - for the year 1870, which shews that, although by reason of improvements in ship building and other causes, the number of casualties has not been so large as in former years, there are still numerous risks and exposures which no human skill or care can guard against, and which must ever be the means of destroying many a gallant vessel. From the statistics we learn that the year 1870 was an exceptionally propitious one, there being fewer severe gales than is usually the case, and, as a consequence the casualties are to a material extent diminished.'

An analysis of the vessels lost was included:

Fishing smacks	83
Colliers, laden	491
Colliers, in ballast	88
Metallic ores	126
Stone ores	115
Ships with other cargoes and other ships in ballast	962
Total	*1865*

'It will be seen that laden colliers, on account of the large number employed in the coasting trade, and the general unseaworthiness of this class of craft, have suffered very severely.

Turning to the sacrifice of human life connected with the above, we find that one wreck in every twelve, on the average, results in loss of life, and that altogether 744 persons were drowned or otherwise deprived of life.'

The article concluded: 'We should, therefore, be glad to see that our local lifeboats are more liberally supported by our local middle-class people.'

The next column contained the following account:

'On Saturday afternoon last, the crew of the lifeboat *Burton-on-Trent* (the property of the National Lifeboat Institution) went out for a quarterly practice, and from the opinions which we heard we learnt that the prejudice which was so rife against her at first has to some extent died out, and great things are expected of her whenever she is needed. So high did the partisanship run when the old boat was presented to the fishermen, that one old man asserted that he "would rather go out in the old boat if he knew he was to be drowned, than go in the new one to be saved."

The general verdict on Saturday was that the *Burton-on-Trent* acquitted herself well, "floated like a duck" over the heavy breakers, and would be of great use in keeping down the number of black dots on the Wreck Chart, which each mark the position of a casualty.

We may state in conclusion that the old boat "the *Zetland*" is entirely under the control of the fishermen, and this being the case she deserves to be liberally supported by the inhabitants of the town, not only for that fact, but also because she is a curiosity, being the oldest lifeboat in the kingdom, having been built in 1802 by Greathead of Sunderland. She has been the means of rescuing upwards of 350 lives, and is now stated to be as sound as when she was built.'

This would seem to be the first contemporary reference to the lifeboat being named *Zetland*.

1872

Meetings were held in June to plan the second Redcar Regatta and it was decided that a prize should be given for a lifeboat race. Joseph Whitwell Pease Esq., a local industrialist, offered a handsome silver cup, value 10 guineas (£10.50), for the best manned, best equipped, and most efficient lifeboat and £5 for the second.

On the 8th July an advertisement in the *Redcar and Saltburn Gazette* proclaimed that the regatta was 'open to the whole of the East coast from the Tyne to the Humber,' and that there would be held 'a life boat rowing race with large or small lifeboats, property of the Royal Life-Boat Institution or belonging to a local committee, requiring a crew of not less than 23 men when fully equipped. All crews to appear as if required to act in a storm. Entrance 10/- [50p], first prize £15, second prize £8, and third prize £4.'

Thursday 18th July was appointed as the great day. Thomas Bland, head teacher of Zetland School, recorded with perhaps a degree of resignation, 'Regatta day - school dismissed at 11 o'clock'. There would have been too much excitement to concentrate on schoolwork, and many of the children would have had fathers or other relatives competing in the events.

Redcar and Saltburn-by-the-Sea Gazette, 19th July:

'REDCAR REGATTA, THE LIFE BOAT RACE

'Redcar was a scene of great excitement yesterday, and for days past the chief topic of conversation has been the projected Regatta. The unsettled condition of the weather and the continued prevalence of north wind and high sea rendering it doubtful whether it would after all take place. The committee could not decide until the last moment, when the weather having abated, it was determined to have the Life Boat Race, the sea being still too high to permit the other races to take place. The shore was lined with a dense crowd of spectators, whilst a select number were admitted to the Redcar pier by ticket, many also availed themselves of the Coatham pier, near which was one of the turning points of the race.

There were four Life Boats present, viz.: The "Zetland" (Redcar), Twenty-three men, W.Upton, cox.; The "Burton-onTrent" (Redcar), R. Dobson, cox.; The "Foresters' Pride" (West Hartlepool), Thirteen men; The "Fishermen's Friend" (Whitby), Thirteen men. Before the race the boats were examined as to their equipments, &c., by Captain Prowse, of Newcastle-on-Tyne, Inspecting Commander of Coastguard, in the absence of Admiral Chaloner; Captain Robertson, Inspecting Officer of the Royal Lifeboat Institution; and Mr J.Bates, Chief Officer of Coast Guard, Coatham, for the purpose of awarding a special prize, value 10 guineas and a second prize, value £3, the gift of J. W. Pease, Esq., M.P. The first prize was adjudged to the "Foresters' Pride", West Hartlepool, and the second to the "Burton-on-Trent", Redcar.

The course rowed was from the Redcar Pier Head round a buoy stationed near Coatham Pier, round the Rock buoy, and back to the Redcar Pier Head, a distance of over three miles. A very good start was effected at 3.36 p.m., but it was evident from the first that the Whitby boat had no chance, in fact it could not be considered to be in the race after the first one hundred yards had been travelled. The "Zetland" took the lead from the first, and on rounding the buoy near Coatham Pier was considerably in advance of the other boats, and it was apparently certain that she would win as her crew were rowing within themselves, and increasing the distance very much, rounding the rock buoy fully a minute before the other boats. Meanwhile it was a great struggle between the "Burton-on-Trent" and the "Foresters' Pride", for the second place, they pulling closely together. After, however, rounding the rock buoy the "Burton-on-Trent" shot ahead of her opponent and maintained that position to the finish.

The "Zetland" passed the pier head three quarters of a minute before the "Burton-on-Trent", and both the boats were greeted with lusty cheers. The race occupied 36 minutes. The first prize, £15; the second prize, £8; and the third £4.

Amongst the spectators present we were glad to see the two oldest patrons of the winning boat, the Earl of Zetland and his brother-in-law, H.W.Yeoman, Esq., to whose liberality and good feeling the old boat owes its very existence. The " Zetland" is the old traditional Life Boat of Redcar, built in 1802, and repaired so often that it is said no portion of the original boat remains. When deemed unseaworthy a few years ago the Royal Lifeboat Institution sent a new boat to Redcar, but the fishermen stuck to their Lifeboat, and by the help of many friends - and foremost amongst them were Lord Zetland and Mr. Yeoman - she was thoroughly repaired, a house built for her, and the old boat in which our fishermen and their fathers have saved so many lives, still glides like a bird o'er the stormy waters, and was the winning boat yesterday. Lord Stratford de Redcliffe, when staying with Lord Zetland, wrote some spirited verses on the old boat, of which we give the last verse:-

"Thine age shall be respected, thy youth perchance restored,

And sires and sons together shall press thy heaving board;

No fear that storms be wanting; and call it old or new,

We'll cheer the boat that's foremost to save a sinking crew".'

It is possible that Henry Walker Yeoman was moved to have the *Zetland* and its shed brightened up as the following entry was made in the account book of T Guy, painter:

Old Lifeboat - Esquir. Yeoman. Sept 8th.

	£	s	d	(kg	£ p)
32 lb of White		18	8	(14.5	93)
6 lb of Oil		3	6	(2.7	17½)
2½ lb of Black		1	5½	(1.1	7½)
3½ lb of Red		2	0¼	(1.6	10)
4 lb of Dark colour		2	4	(1.8	11½)
Metcalfe, 4 days	1	0	0	(	1.00)
Self, 4 days	1	4	0	(	1.20)
Paid	*3*	*12*	*0*	(	*3.60*)

Life Boat House - Sept 11th

	£	s	d	(kg	£ p)
3 lb of Black		1	9	(1.4	9)
10 lb of Drab		3	10	(4.5	19)
5 lb Oil		2	11	(2.3	14)
Metcalfe, 4 days	1	0	0		
Paid	*1*	*10*	*6*		

The census for 1871 shows that Thomas Guy, a thirty-five year old painter, lived at 4 Bath Street, Redcar, and employed two men. He charged 6d (2½p) per hour and paid his men 5d per hour.

1873

The old lifeboat lost a generous benefactor on the 6th May with the death of Thomas, second Earl of Zetland, at his home at Aske Hall, Richmond. He had been all but disabled from walking for a few years as the result of an accident. As soon as news of his death reached Redcar the flag was flown at half-mast from the look-out at Fishermans Square. The funeral was at noon on Tuesday the 13th and was attended by a large number of local people. The body of Lord Zetland had been conveyed by train from Richmond to Marske and arrived at 11.30 am. A hearse and mourning coaches waited at the station and proceeded slowly through the village to the old church of St Germains. All places of business in Marske were closed and the bells of the new church rang muffled peals. The service was conducted by the Rev T Robson, and the coffin, covered in rich crimson velvet and surmounted by the earl's coronet, was borne by eight members of the estate from Aske Hall and Upleatham. At Redcar, businesses were closed between 11am and 2pm, the school was closed, and the minute bell tolled. A large number of townsfolk attended the funeral, and included the fishermen who had not gone to sea that day as a mark of respect.

Lord Zetland was interred in the family vault by the side of St Germains Church. He had been a benevolent man and amongst his good works he had paid for the school at Redcar (1859), given ground for a cemetery and £1,300 towards appropriate buildings (1872), and borne the greater part of the expense of the new church of St Marks at Marske (1867). In 1864 he had given help to the old lifeboat when it had been most needed.

On Whit Monday, the 2nd June, the new pier at Redcar was officially opened and gave cause for great celebration. The ceremony was to have been performed by Admiral Chaloner but owing to him being ill it was performed by Mrs Emma Dawson of Weston Hall, Otley. Accounts of the occasion mention both lifeboats, old and new.

The *Redcar and Saltburn-by-the-Sea Gazette*:

'At this time, the scene on sea and land was of the most pleasing character; on sea the two Redcar life-boats were fully manned and equipped for the occasion, and numerous pleasure boats studded the bay. To the east the volunteer artillery corps were assembled for big gun practice, to the west the shore and Esplanade were crowded with spectators, most of whom visited the pier during the day. The bathing-machines plying their trade added to the liveliness of the scene, and in the distance, Coatham Pier, which was decorated with flags, completed the coup d'oeil, which was of a picturesque and inspiring description.'

The *Redcar and Saltburn News*:

'Both piers gay with bunting seem to be celebrating the engineers triumph over the waves. Brittania is ruling her waves in more ways than the ancient time honoured one. Those two Redcar Life-boats show one very noble way and those two piers a very pleasant one.'

1874

The *Redcar and Saltburn-by-the-Sea Gazette*, the 20th March:

'Perilous Position of Three Fishing Cobles and Their Crews at Redcar
On Saturday morning last, (14th), three fishing cobles belonging to Redcar,

three men in each boat, whilst pursuing their ordinary avocation, had a very narrow escape from being lost at sea. From what we can gather it appears that when the boats put off in the morning, about five o'clock, the sea was comparatively smooth; but before long a great change was experienced, which placed the boats and their crews in imminent danger, and it was soon evident that if some aid was not speedily forthcoming, a sad loss of life would have occurred.

The drum went round, and the old life-boat - the "Redcar", the heroic deeds of which were happily recorded in verse by Lord Stratford de Redcliffe, when on a visit to the late Earl of Zetland, at Upleatham - was speedily manned, and put to sea on her errand of mercy. The swell by this time - ten o'clock - was tremendous, frequently shutting out the life-boat and the cobles from the anxious gaze of a large number of spectators who lined the beach and the Redcar pier, and who awaited the result with breathless anticipation.

The life-boat nobly did its work, and succeeded in getting all the crews of the cobles on board, and returned them safe and sound - save for being very cold and wet - to the arms of their anxious wives and relatives, who were congregated on the shore. Fortunately, the wind was blowing from the land, had such not been the case we should in all probability have had to record in our columns a similar catastrophe as that which befell the poor fishermen of Cresswell last week; as it was, the situation was one of extreme peril.'

(The incident at Cresswell occurred on the 9th March when four fishermen, a father and three sons, were drowned when their coble capsized. It led to a successful appeal to the RNLI for a lifeboat to be stationed at the village.)

The *Redcar and Saltburn-by-the-Sea Gazette*, the 6th November:

'Mr W.Potts has received a donation of £10 towards the old life-boat fund from the Hon. Mrs Ramsden, daughter of the 1st Lord Dundas who gave the life-boat to Redcar. The donation was paid over to Mr Potts by H.W.Yeoman of Marske Hall, chief patron and friend of the old boat so loved by Redcar fishermen.'

The *Redcar and Saltburn-by-the-Sea Gazette*, the 11th December:

'The heavy gale which swept over the United Kingdom was felt with especial severity on the north-east coast. No storm of such violence having visited this coast since the well-known Whitsuntide storm of 1860, when twelve sailing vessels and one steamer were wrecked between the Tees and Saltburn. The storm arose about midnight on Tuesday, and raged with terrific violence till Wednesday morning (9th). Many people in Redcar, besides the fishermen, were aroused about four o'clock, and witnessed the scene on the beach.

Thomas Picknett was the first to raise the alarm, he was up late, or rather being early attending to the safety of his boats, when he saw a vessel drifting over Saltscar rocks, and he at once called the attention of the Coastguard on watch thereto. After which he proceeded to rouse the fishermen by beating the "tattoo" on the lifeboat drum. In attempting to launch the new lifeboat the combined action of the wind and surf stove in the boat, and she could not be used. The new lifeboat was taken out because it was nearer the scene of distress than the old boat, and the fishermen were willing to give it a fair trial. It has had this, and at least in this instance was a failure.'

The vessel in distress proved to be the brig *Garibaldi*, of Cowes, which washed over Saltscar and stranded near Coatham pier. Her Captain and crew were saved by rocket apparatus under the command of Mr Bates, chief officer of the coastguard.

The brig *Griffin* was driven through Coatham pier and her crew leapt onto the pier for safety.

The schooner *Corrymbus* was also driven through Coatham pier but her crew stayed on board until the tide had receded and left their vessel high and dry.

The crew of the brigantine *Express*, ashore to the east of Redcar, were saved and the crew of the *Robert and William*, ashore on Coatham sands, waited for the tide to leave their vessel high and dry.

1875

The *Zetland* lost another great friend and benefactor when Henry Walker Yeoman died at the age of eighty-six. He had always taken a keen interest in local matters and the welfare of the area. As an enthusiastic diarist he had observed much on his regular walks between Redcar and his home at Marske Hall.

His funeral took place on the 21st September and such was his popularity that it was one of the largest known at Marske. Squire Yeoman was buried close by the east wall of the churchyard of St Germains next to his wife, Margaret Bruce, sister of Thomas, second Earl of Zetland, and daughter of Lawrence, the first earl. A measure of the esteem in which he had been held can be found in an account of his death in the *Redcar and Saltburn-by-the-Sea Gazette*: 'It may truly be said he died beloved, revered, and lamented'.

1876

Veteran fisherman and lifeboatman James Metcalfe was drowned on the 6th August whilst attending to Cmdr Watt's coble anchored half a mile off Redcar. A poem by George J Robinson paid tribute to Metcalfe's lifeboat career and was published in the *Redcar and Saltburn-by-the-Sea Gazette* in September. He had been a member of the crew of the *Zetland* and wrecks mentioned in the verses included the barque *Emma* (1857), and the *Emily* (1876). A brief paragraph beneath the poem reminded readers that 'The widow of James

The brig Griffin *after she had been driven through Coatham pier during a gale on the 9th December 1874. Brigs were one of the most common types of coasting vessels and great fleets of them transported coal from the North-East. Many were blown ashore or sunk during gales and the* Zetland *was involved in at least thirty-two rescues from this type of vessel. (Photograph by courtesy of Kirkleatham Old Hall Museum.)*

Metcalfe is advanced in years, in bad health, and indigent circumstances. Subscriptions on her behalf will be received at the office of this paper'.

The Redcar and Saltburn-by-the-Sea Gazette, the 25th August.

'Lifeboat Service at Redcar

On Wednesday evening (23rd), between eight and nine o'clock, the old lifeboat was launched to the aid of three men who had gone out in the early part of the afternoon for the purpose of marking for the Artillery Volunteer, they being unable to get back in consequence of the heavy sea that was running, which made their position very dangerous. The men were taken on board the lifeboat and brought ashore, little the worse for their exposure, amidst much cheering from an immense crowd which had congregated on the beach'.

The Redcar and Saltburn-by-the-Sea Gazette, the 8th September.

'Another ship ashore at Redcar

The North German brig "Stafftte" (Edward Perrow, master), of Memel, bound for Hartlepool with timber and deals, struck on the rocks called the Flashes, east of Redcar Pier, on Monday morning (4th) shortly before eight o'clock, it being a little over half low water, ebb tide. The place where the ship struck is within 200 yards of the spot where the North German brigantine "Odor" was stranded a fortnight ago last Saturday, but which was successfully got off, and now lies at Middlesbrough undergoing repairs.

The "Stafftte", which is 76 years old, left Memel on the 3rd August, with eight hands on board, and has experienced rough weather in the North Sea, there being 10 feet of water in her hold, notwithstanding that her pumps had been kept working day and night. The cause of her stranding is attributable to the fact of the vessel being in such a leaky state that the Captain was obliged to keep close to the shore.

The crew of the old lifeboat at Redcar, "the Zetland", was got together, and the boat having been launched, was speedily got off to the stranded vessel, and the whole of the crew were taken off, with their chests, and etc.

Contrary to all expectations, the ship was got off in the afternoon, and towed to her destination, accompanied by the old lifeboat.'

At the annual meeting of the governing body of United Free Gardeners, held at West Bromwich in June, it was resolved to have a lifeboat constructed and stationed at Redcar. The suggestion had been made the previous year at the annual grand meeting in Newcastle.

The reasons given for the unanimous choice of Redcar were that wrecks in the area were frequent and the RNLI lifeboat was considered unsuitable because of its straight keel. (The keel of the *Zetland* was curved and considered to give the boat more manoeuvrability.) The RNLI lifeboat could be removed to a place more suited to its build and the vacated boat-house could be used by the Free Gardeners for their boat.

'No place was better situated for access by rail if the United Free Gardeners wished to come and see their boat launched. Owing to the number of members of the society at Redcar, the new lifeboat could be manned exclusively by United Free Gardeners.' (The Marine Lodge of the society had been formed at Redcar in 1862.)

On the 16th September a deputation from the Marine Lodge met with the Tees Bay committee of the RNLI and stated the intention of their parent society to have a lifeboat built and to present it to the RNLI. The lifeboat committee resolved that 'the worthy and much valued offer be forwarded to the RNLI, with the recommendation that this honourable donation be thankfully received'.

Further discussion about the offer made by the United Free Gardeners took place at a meeting at the Royal Hotel on Saturday the 23rd September. Admiral Robertson, one of the lifeboat inspectors of the RNLI, met with a number of fishermen and pilots of Redcar. A very strong opinion was expressed by the latter parties in favour of a lifeboat of a similar design to the *Zetland*. They considered the RNLI boat *Burton-on-Trent* too heavy for launching from Redcar beach and much less manageable than the *Zetland*, which was still

The lifeboat of The United Order of Free Gardeners stationed at Redcar in 1877. Such was the confidence in the Zetland *that when she was discarded by the RNLI the fishermen demanded a replacement of the same design. When the RNLI refused, the United Order of Free Gardeners met the expense of providing a similar boat. She was built by Jackson of South Shields at a cost of £600 and was slightly larger than the* Zetland *at 33 feet (10.05 m) long by 11 feet (3.35 m) in the beam. (Photograph by courtesy of Kirkleatham Old Hall Museum.)*

retained by them.Admiral Robertson suggested as a compromise that the *Burton-on-Trent* be retained and, if the RNLI accepted the offer of the United Free Gardeners, then their boat could be built on the old principle as a replacement for the *Zetland*. It was the general opinion that the old boat had nearly done her work and that an understanding be reached between the fishermen and the RNLI, so that there would be two efficient lifeboats at Redcar, one on the old principle and one of the self-righting design.

During the early hours of Wednesday the 20th December, a terrific storm began to blow from between south-east and east-south-east. It reached its height in the early hours of Thursday and immense seas washed away the upper part of Coatham pier head, including the landing stage and lighthouse.

The *Redcar and Saltburn-by-the-Sea Gazette* reported that between three and four o'clock during the afternoon of the same day, 'A two masted schooner was descried in the vicinity of the volunteer battery. The waves broke over her half mast high, and she was momentarily expected to strike. The new lifeboat "Burton-on-Trent" was got out, and taken near the spot, and the crew of the

THE LIFEBOAT
PRESENTED BY THE BOROUGH
OF BURTON-ON-TRENT, STATIONED
AT REDCAR, BUT NOW OUT
OF SERVICE.

From a Photograph taken at
Messrs. Worthington & Co's Brewery,
45 years ago.

The Burton-on-Trent *was typical of self-righting lifeboats built for the RNLI in the second half of the nineteenth century. At first the design was disliked intensely by the fishermen and pilots of Redcar. Experience gradually overcame their prejudice and in 1884, when the* Burton-on-Trent *was condemned unfit for further service, one lifeboatman claimed 'that there never was and never would be a boat to equal her'. A few die-hards were never won over and supported the* Zetland *with tenacious loyalty. (From a postcard in a private collection.)*

old lifeboat held themselves in readiness, but, contrary to all expectations, the schooner managed to get clear of the rocks and disappeared as night closed in.'

1877

On the 9th March an editorial appeared in the *Redcar and Saltburn-by-the-Sea Gazette* in criticism of the disagreement over the type of lifeboat to be stationed at Redcar. An account of the meeting of the 23rd September 1876 was repeated, when the local wish had been to substitute the Free Gardeners lifeboat for the *Burton-on-Trent*. Admiral Robertson had considered the proposal 'inadmissible', on the ground that the people of Burton-on-Trent had subscribed for and given the boat to Redcar, and its removal would be an insult and breach of faith on the part of the RNLI to the donors.

The newspaper commented that the Free Gardeners seemed determined to present their boat to Redcar, and Redcar only, and speculated as to whether it would replace the *Zetland*, or be a second independent lifeboat:

'... thus, in place of settling the old dispute ... there will be three lifeboats at Redcar which will practically hand on to posterity the feuds and bickerings amongst the rival supporters, which all who are well affected towards the Redcar fishermen wish to die out.'

A brief account was given of how the *Zetland* had been discarded as unseaworthy by the RNLI and later put into satisfactory repair by public subscription.

'It would appear that the old boat had not been put into such thorough repair as was expected, for signs of decay are now apparent, and it is of the opinion of some persons qualified to judge that the old boat has now done her work, and that henceforth her place should be monumental.'

The United Free Gardeners pressed ahead and bought their lifeboat. It was built by Jackson of South Shields and was of similar design to the *Zetland* although slightly larger.

The naming ceremony took place at Redcar on the 30th July and attracted a massive crowd. At least 20,000 arrived by excursion trains and many more by steamers from Newcastle, Sunderland, Whitby, and Hartlepool. The lifeboat was given pride of place in a procession that included several bands and representatives of the many lodges of Free Gardeners.

An unfortunate incident occurred in High Street when the spokes gave way on the wheels of the new lifeboat carriage and the procession was obliged to continue without its principal attraction. A long delay followed whilst the boat was transferred to the carriage from the *Zetland*. Once mobile again, she was taken onto the sands and named *United Free Gardener* by Mrs Emma Dawson of Weston Hall, Otley.

1880-1889

1880

From 1am on Thursday the 28th October 1880 a terrific storm blew from the east-north-east and was accompanied by heavy rain. Much structural damage was done and the force of the wind combined with floods to cause great disruption to the day to day routine of the area.

The headteacher of Zetland School, W Harrison, entered in the log: 'A fearful storm raging. Several ships ashore - the result is that so few children have turned up that it is of no use opening the school.'

The columns of the *Redcar and Saltburn-by-the-Sea Gazette* were given over to stories of the storm. The first accounts had been written on Thursday and had been updated as news came to hand. Publication day was Saturday 30th.

Thursday:

'The storm has been raging all night, and is now raging with great fierceness at Redcar. The streets are literally strewn with slates, red tiles, chimney pots, and other debris; and the great majority of the shops are "shuttered," as it is utterly impossible to transact business. The huge waves are beating heavily against the promenade, which is covered with surf. A large number of people have arrived from Middlesbrough, Stockton, and adjacent district; and considerable amusement is afforded by the endeavours of venturesome spirits to reach Coatham pier and other points of vantage from which a good view of the sea can be obtained.

The schooner *Luna*, 99 tons burden, owned by Mr John Crosby, of Sunderland, left Leamington for Sunderland on Monday last, and has encountered very severe weather. At ten o'clock this morning she was driven to a point at Coatham opposite Warrenby furnaces. The vessel - manned by four hands, - was observed to be in distress and at half past ten the *Free Gardeners'* lifeboat, under the captaincy of Coxswain Picknett, was shoved off to the vessel, from which the crew was safely rescued, and removed to the Globe Hotel, where they are now staying. A rocket was fired from the beach, but the line broke. The sails of the vessel are all blown away, but there seems no doubt that she will soon be righted.

The brig *Emanuel Boutcher* (eight hands), 181 tons burden, owned by Mr Wm Walker, of Whitby, is rapidly becoming a total wreck about half a mile south-east of Redcar. Last Saturday week she commenced a voyage from Rotterdam to Whitby. Having made a stay at Yarmouth Roads, she proceeded on her voyage on Tuesday morning, and suffered from the effects of a severe gale. At six o'clock this morning the brig "struck". This was observed by a fisherman named Thomas Baker, who was standing in Fisherman's Square. He quickly gave the alarm ; and the *Burton-on-Trent* lifeboat was speedily rowed to the scene by twenty three men.

Five rockets were fired from the shore. Four missed fire altogether; and one struck the rigging. The crew however, found it utterly impossible to reach the rope, and they anxiously awaited the arrival of the *Burton-on-Trent*. The lifeboat - with the coxswain Joseph Burnicle at the head - soon gained the vessel, and the crew were soon taken from the brig, which was half-filled with water, and as we have said, will soon become a wreck. The crew were removed to the Stockton Hotel. The rocket firing was superintended by Mr Browney, skipper of the coastguard; and Mr J H D Taplin rendered invaluable service in getting the lifeboat away to the distressed vessel.

It is stated by very old residents of Redcar that they can remember nothing to equal the severity of the gale, and the noble way in which the Redcar lifeboatmen have done their duty - having been instrumental in saving twelve lives - speaks well for the unflinching courage of our Redcar fishermen.

This afternoon the screw steamer *Tees* of Middlesbrough, while making for the Tees, was driven onto the Redcar Sands, the sea making a clean breach over her. Great excitement prevailed, the promenade being crowded with spectators from Middlesbrough and the district. The life-brigade men were promptly on the spot, and were fortunately more successful than in the early part of the day, for they were able to rescue the whole of the crew by the apparatus. As the benumbed and half-drowned seamen were pulled safely along the line cheer after cheer was raised. The poor fellows who had so narrowly escaped a watery grave were well cared for.'

Friday:

'The gale continued until last night with terrific fury. At nine o'clock in the evening lights were shown from a distressed vessel on the rocks, between the piers. An alarm was given by Thomas Picknett of the Free Gardeners' Lifeboat-house.

The lifeboat was again got ready for action and the rocket apparatus was at once on the spot. Lights were exhibited from the shore, but the vessel broke away from the rocks and drove in shore, when it was found that she had parted in two, leaving only the stern. A rocket was fired over the vessel, but there being no place to make fast the line, no help could be rendered in this way. The lifeboat could not be launched, the horses being unable to make a start.

The shouts from those on the vessel were truly heart-rending. However, the tide returned enough for a line to be thrown to the wreck, and the fishermen were ready to save, if possible, the poor helpless men. Some time elapsed before this could be done, and by the aid of lines, the crew, twelve in number, were safely landed and taken to the Swan Hotel, where they were taken care of by Mr Rogowski. This vessel turned out to be the barque *Minna*, of Enno, Capt. Fisher, in ballast from London to Newcastle.

Early this morning, (Friday 29th), another sign of distress was exhibited from a vessel crossing the rocks to the east of Redcar Pier. The Old Lifeboat, *Zetland* was made ready for launching. The vessel had by this time drifted helplessly in the direction of the centre of the pier, and fears were entertained as to the safety of the pier. Unfortunately the strong wind and the sweeping tide forced the vessel through the pier without stoppage.

The pier now stands divided in the centre, and about fifty yards has fallen into the sea. The deck of the pier fell upon the vessel as she passed through, but luckily all hands were down below. The sudden crash caused the men to come on deck, and they had to cling to the wreck to save themselves from being washed overboard - the huge breakers rolling completely over her. Many people were on the pier but a few yards from the stranded vessel, but could not help them. The rocket brigade had fired all their rockets, and the scene was most affecting.

The *Zetland* was launched for the first time, and succeeded in reaching the disabled vessel, taking on board the whole of the crew, seven in number. [The RNLI awarded £10 to the crew of the *Zetland* for this rescue.] It was the brig *Luna*, of Rochester, Capt. Frend, of that port, in ballast, from Rochester to Shields. It is reported, when out at sea, he ordered the masts of his vessel to be cut down in order to save themselves.

The wreckage of a Dutch Galliot has washed ashore on the Coatham beach, supposed to have foundered at sea during the night. A fine large barque is reported ashore in the Tees. At Saltburn a rumour is afloat that a screw steamer has gone down with all hands.

About eleven o'clock (Friday morning) another brig was observed flying a flag of distress, and labouring heavily under a little canvas near East-scar end, and the lifeboat *Burton-on-Trent* was again drawn in the direction of the brig, which ran ashore near Marske, the lifeboat was launched, and the Saltburn rocket brigade fired two shots over the vessel, but the crew were unable to use the apparatus. The lifeboat was pulled out to the vessel and in a few minutes the crew of nine were taken on board the lifeboat and landed, they were conveyed to Redcar, when they were received by Mr Skinner, Stockton Hotel.

This is believed to be the brig John and Mary *which was driven ashore at Saltburn on the 28th October 1880 by the same storm in which the Zetland made her last rescue. The brig was bound from Portsmouth to Sunderland in ballast. Her crew made their way ashore at low water. (Photograph by courtesy of Kirkleatham Old Hall Museum.)*

This was the brig *Hazard*, Capt. Anson, from Dover to Norway in ballast. This was the fifth crew in which the Redcar lifeboat men and life brigade had been instrumental in saving, the total number of lives saved being forty-seven. This speaks well for the Redcar lifeboat men.'

(An account published seventeen years later claimed that the *Burton-on-Trent* had a hole stove in her side whilst being launched to the *Minna*. It was also claimed that as the *Free Gardeners* lifeboat was being launched to the schooner *Luna*, the carriage became embedded in the sand and had to be dug out the next day. No reference to the accidents has been traced in contemporary accounts, including those of the RNLI. Perhaps the passage of time led to some confusion of the facts. It was also stated of the *Minna* that 'a pig belonging to the ill fated vessel washed ashore alive on Coatham sands and was taken care of'. That fact was far less open to dispute!)

W Harrison entered in the log for Zetland School:

'29th October. The storm yesterday was the most fearful known for many years. No fewer than six vessels now lie stranded within a comparatively short distance of each other, one of them having been blown clean through Redcar pier. The result to the school may be readily imagined. Although the morning is beautifully fine 90 children only in attendance the rest being employed in gathering wreckage on the beach and I know from experience that so long as there remains any wreckage or sea coal on the beach the chances of our getting a good attendance are but slight indeed.

When to this is added the fact that several more children are this morning reported as being attacked with measles, things on this last day of the school year are looking very gloomy. Under the circumstances the managers have deemed it advisable to ask Mr Callender to postpone the examination.'

Captain W B Friend, owner and master of the brig *Luna*, gave an account in the *Redcar and Saltburn-by-the-Sea Gazette* of the 6th November of how he came to be shipwrecked. He and his crew had been rescued by the *Zetland*. In a statement to a reporter he told of the onset of the gale and how the sails had blown out one by one. On the Thursday morning the foretopmast had gone over the side and carried away the jibboom. Thinking that the remainder of the foremast and the mainmast might also come down and do great damage he ordered them to be cut away. The anchor was let go and needed about 150 fathoms (274 metres) of chain to halt the drift of the brig. It held for about three hours then parted.

'We then showed about twenty "flares" before she struck on the tail end of Redcar rocks. She struck three times very heavily, and came over and drove right through the pier about half past twelve. She took part of the pier with her on her decks, where it is now to be seen. Nobody was struck except myself, for the men were in the cabin, where I gave them orders to remain until I told them to come on deck. Well, the ironwork came right through the after part of the companion and although it went through the cabin none of the men, as I say, were struck. I ordered the men on deck. We saw the men trying to assist us; but when we saw that their efforts were useless, we remained on the top of the "pier," which fell on the deck, and held fast by the rails for three or four hours, when we were taken off, and removed to this [the Swan] hotel.

The vessel was as strong as wood and iron could make her, or she could not have withstood the gale. During the three hours we were clinging to the rails tons and tons of water rolled over us. I am rather severely hurt about the ankle, but I don't intend to call in a doctor, as the good lady has had hospital experience, and has almost brought me round. The rest of the crew will soon be right again.'

The following letter appeared on the same date as the narrative of Captain Friend:

'REDCAR LIFEBOATMEN

"GENTLEMEN, -

During the terrific gale on Thursday last I was one of the many spectators on the beach here. Between ten and eleven p.m. the rocket apparatus commenced to throw rockets to the German barque *Minna*, which had struck very near to Coatham Pier. Twelve rockets seem to be the supply allowed to each station, and as they had used most of them during the day to other ships in distress, they had only four or five left, which were all thrown without success. When the fact became known that there were no more rockets, the spectators raised a cry for the lifeboats.

At that time there was another ship, the brig *Luna*, showing lights for assistance, and shortly after she came right through Redcar Pier. The lifeboatmen could not be persuaded to go off. At last several of the spectators went and took possession of the lifeboat, and pulled it to the beach, where it stuck fast in the sand.

Four horses were then brought, but the owner would not allow them to be used owing to some difference of opinion with the lifeboatmen. They cavilled on for a long time, until there was not sufficient water for it to reach the wreck. A coble was then proposed, and after another considerable delay one was brought, but that was of no use. At this time the cries of the poor fellows on the wreck, which was fast breaking up, were fearful.

It was then a few brave fellows - Mr Wm Previll, butcher; Mr Umpleby, tailor; Mr E Moore, a fisherman named Wm Carter, myself, and one or two others walked through the surf holding each other's hands, and got sufficiently near the wreck to speak to the men, who said if they were not speedily saved they would all be washed away, as they were so very weak. We returned and asked the lifeboatmen for the loan of a line; but they refused, saying it was impossible to do anything for them, and that as they had waited so long it would do them no harm to stay a bit longer.

After throwing every obstacle in our way, they at last let us have a rope. The same party again went in, the rope was thrown, luckily caught and made fast, by which means the crew and a North Sea pilot, of London, were all saved. The latter, an old man of sixty-eight years of age, afterwards complained that all his things were stolen from the wreck. The captain of the vessel says he could not have imagined any Englishmen acting as the lifeboatmen did. Cowardice is a hard word to use against such men, but it is the only one that can be applied to them, and the matter deserves to be made public.

> Yours respectfully,
> HUMANITY."

The above letter appeared in the "Echo" on Thursday morning, and we trust that the coxswains of the Redcar lifeboats *Burton-on-Trent* and *Emma* will speak on behalf of their crews and themselves.'

After more than a century it is impossible to tell how much, if any, justification there was in the criticism of the lifeboatmen. As they had already rescued eleven that day and went on to rescue a further sixteen the following day there would seem to have been no justification at all. Perhaps 'Humanity' was ignorant of the ways of the coast and mistook the actions of reasoned judgement for apathy. An article in defence of the lifeboatmen and a somewhat different version of the *Minna* incident was published in the *Redcar and Saltburn-by-the-Sea Gazette* of the 13th November:

'THE RECENT STORM, AND THE REDCAR LIFEBOATMEN

It is said by the oldest fishermen of Redcar, that never was there such a destructive gale to shipping and property on the East coast as that which visited this district on the 28th ult. Eight vessels were driven ashore on the beach within a reach of seven miles. [A brief account followed of how the crews had been rescued from the *Emanuel Boutcher*, the *Luna* and the *Tees.*] About ten o'clock the German Barque *Minna* struck the rocks called West Scar. All the rockets had been fired during the storm, and the *Burton-on-Trent* was again called for service, but some time elapsed before she arrived. The crew, assisted by many landsmen pulled the boat by the aid of ropes along the Esplanade, and on touching the beach the sand was found to be very soft, and the men were unable to draw the boat further - the wheels of the boat's carriage very soon became embedded in the sand - the horses had by this time reached the spot. The crew were again seated ready for launching, but the horses were also unable to move the lifeboat, even when the crew got out and assisted them.

The tide had returned sufficiently for the vessel to be reached by the aid of ropes, and the crew were taken from the wreck in a perishing condition. There still remained another wreck to be attended to near Redcar pier, and the lifeboatmen were again hurried off immediately to rescue the crew of the Rochester brig. The *Zetland* had to be launched amongst the rocks, and there was great difficulty in reaching the vessel - this crew was also saved. At noon the *Burton-on-Trent* was drawn for the third time, in the direction of Marske, to the rescue of the Norwegian brig - once more all hands were rescued, amidst the ringing cheers of the assembled crowd. The large number of lives saved by the Redcar fishermen during the severe storm is a fitting answer to those letters in the local papers which cast imputations upon the character for gallantry which the Redcar fishermen have so long borne.'

A letter dated the 12th November from the master of the *Minna* to the *Redcar and Saltburn-by-the-Sea Gazette* would also seem to refute the accusations made by 'Humanity':

'Royal Hotel, Redcar.

Sir,

Before leaving Redcar for Germany I am desirous to express my deep gratitude for the kindness and sympathy shown to my crew and myself by the inhabitants of Redcar. As most of those brave men who helped to rescue us from the perilous position on the wreck remain unknown to me, I can thank them only through the medium of your paper and hope you will be good enough to insert this letter.

Yours respectfully,

O. Fischer.'

Inquests were held along the coast as the unfortunate victims of the storm began to wash ashore. The bodies of a man and boy were laid in a loft in the Ship Inn, Saltburn, to await an inquest. Whilst the enquiry was in session another body was found on the shore and brought to the inn. The district coroner, Mr Arthur Buchannan, remarked that it was to be much regretted that there was no public mortuary in a place like Saltburn, it being so desirable for any bodies washed ashore to be kept above ground as long as possible, so as to afford every opportunity for their being identified.

The following year a mortuary was built across the road from the Ship Inn and still stands today. It has outlasted the lifeboat house and the store for the rocket brigade equipment that once stood in line with it.

The crew of the *Luna* were the last to be rescued by the *Zetland*. No record has been found that she ever took to the water again. For the next decade the old lifeboat would seem to have remained in her shed - out of sight but never out of mind.

1890-1899

1891

19th September, the *Redcar and Saltburn-by-the-Sea Gazette*:

'A procession of two lifeboats and their crews, rocket brigade, and fire engines paraded from the Esplanade through the main streets to raise funds for the RNLI. £16 4s (£16.20) was collected along the route. The RNLI lifeboat was then launched and went through some useful exercises.'

The other lifeboat mentioned was almost certainly the *Zetland*. A little over two months before the lifeboat parade - the 6th July - the following was minuted at a meeting of the Redcar Local Board:

'Moved by Mr. Hudson, seconded by Mr. Brown, and carried unanimously, that the Chairman (George Hood) and Messrs. Shieldon and Kirton be appointed a committee to ascertain upon what terms the old lifeboat can be obtained and as to fixing and placing same in the triangular piece of land at the east end of Redcar.'

It was the start of fifteen years of uncertainty as to where a resting place for the *Zetland* could be found. Many sites were to be suggested but none would seem to have been wholly suitable. The reasons used against some sites have survived in council minutes and newspaper reports, whilst the reasons against other places went unrecorded and have been long forgotten. Finance, or lack of it, was most likely the deciding factor in many instances.

That the *Zetland* would be preserved there was no doubt: the loyalty of the townspeople guaranteed that.

1893

28th January, *Redcar and Saltburn News*:

'The Old Life-Boat at Redcar, which has found a shelter for many years in a rickety old building at the east end of Redcar, will shortly require a new habitation, and we trust it will secure a better and more suitable one. The

Redcar Esplanade photographed from the pier by Guisborough photographer George Page around 1900. The Free Gardeners lifeboat house, now home of the Zetland, is the third tall building from the left and the RNLI lifeboat house is five buildings beyond. (Photograph by courtesy of Kirkleatham Old Hall Museum.)

building which has sheltered it in recent years has to come down, and it will be necessary, if the old boat is to be preserved from utter destruction, to find another site for it.

Surely therefore the present generation can find it an honourable position where it could be seen by fishermen, visitors and others who would be reminded of bygone days and the gallant deeds which it and the brave fishermen of a past age took part.

It has been suggested that it should be placed on the Esplanade; and protected in some structure where it could be seen and yet preserved from decay. We have no doubt many people would willingly subscribe towards a feasible scheme for the preservation of the Old Life-Boat, and no doubt if the facts were brought before the Lord of the Manor, the Marquis of Zetland, he would liberally render assistance toward the object named.'

On the 18th March the *Redcar and Saltburn-by-the-Sea Gazette* reported a meeting of the Redcar Local Board held two days earlier. Members had met with Mr Moscrop, agent of the Zetland estate, with regard to a suitable site for public lavatories.

A photograph taken by T H Nelson whilst the Zetland was being restored and repainted for the Lifeboat Saturday parade in Huddersfield (arrangements were later changed and the Zetland was not needed). The photograph was produced for sale as a postcard by the Redcar and Saltburn News. *T H Nelson continued his interest in the old boat and was recorded as a member of the* Zetland *Lifeboat Committee in 1907.*
(From a postcard in a private collection.)

'The subject of a site for the Old Lifeboat was also discussed, and Mr. Moscrop intimated that it had been suggested to put it in the Poundfold. The party visited the Old Lifeboathouse and inspected "the boat with a history". The majority were of the opinion that the site named was very suitable.'

(At that period the poundfold, or cattle pen, would seem to have been on the landward side of Lord Street, between South Terrace and the land on which William Street now stands.)

14th April, *Redcar and Saltburn-by-the-Sea Gazette*:

'We understand a meeting of the fishermen was held last night, at which it was resolved to erect a building on the Esplanade, where the old lifeboat may probably find a home.'

At a meeting of the Redcar Local Board on the 4th September it was moved by the chairmen, G Hood, seconded by Mr Wetherald and carried (Mr Hudson against) 'that the plan of the proposed shed to be erected for the old lifeboat be rejected on the ground of it being an obstruction.' It is not clear which of the proposed sites was rejected but it would seem to have been the one on the Esplanade.

Amongst mementoes in the watch house of the South Shields Volunteer Life-Brigade are two cuttings from the *Shields Gazette* and *Shipping Telegraph*. They give details of Greathead's lifeboats and a history of the *Zetland* accompanied by the comment 'There are those who think it should be at South Shields. Perhaps the council (at Shields) might find it worth their while to approach the Lord Zetland on the matter'.

1894

A comprehensive history of the *Zetland* , compiled by 'An Old Stager', was serialised in the *Redcar and Saltburn-by-the-Sea Gazette* over the 2nd, 9th, 16th and 23rd June.

In the same month the *Redcar and Saltburn News* reported:

'The Redcar old lifeboat has been repainted and looks quite smart for its intended journey to Huddersfield for the annual Life-Boat Saturday in that town. A good photograph of the old Life-Boat has been taken and we are preparing at this office a copper photo engraving plate from it, by which means cheap copies of the photograph may be obtained, and doubtless many will be glad of the opportunity of possessing a likeness of this most interesting relic of bygone days.'

The photograph sold for 3d (approx 1½p) and had been taken by Mr T Nelson and printed by George Hood, publisher of the *Redcar and Saltburn News*.

It transpired that the *Zetland* was not required at Huddersfield, a rebuff that was recorded with indignation on the 22nd June:

'Positive information has arrived at Redcar from Yorkshire that the old *Zetland* Lifeboat "is not wanted". It appears that the Lifeboat Saturdays at Huddersfield and Dewsbury, are to be managed more economically, by combining, and securing the same lifeboats for each town, to save the expense of transmission from Redcar &c. Thus, after several weeks' labour in painting, forcing, breaking, unscrewing rusty bolts in the carriage, which has been entombed for thirty years in a damp, dark dungeon, opinions differ, as to whether the oldest existing lifeboat would not have been more attractive in Yorkshire than those of modern construction.

During the process of renovation, crowds of aged and infirm neighbours have visited the scene, anxious to gaze once more upon their old friend-in-need, when all others failed, and repeat the oft-told stories of their fathers and grandfathers. So far as the *Zetland* lifeboat is concerned, her career is closed:-"The light of other days has faded, And all her glories past." But her Deeds Live in Hearts that loved her well, and they grace Britannia's story.'

It is probable that this photograph formed the basis for an engraving of the
Zetland *at sea that appeared in* The Book of the Lifeboat, *published in 1894.*
There are at least two lists that claim to identify those on board yet each
differs. The most reliable would seem to be that given by Thomas Hood
Picknett *to Hugh Cook for an article in the* Cleveland Standard *in 1909. He*
was amongst those on board and listed the others as: John Walton (cox),
Willie Carter, Tom Carter, George Dobson, Willie Dobson, Sam Upton, Willie
Potts, Tom Boagey, Jack Picknett Snr, Jack Atkinson, Kit Dobson, John
Walton Jnr, Jim Thompson, and Will Preston. The man on the horse he
identified as 'old Squire Yeoman's coachman'. Names included in the other
list are Robson, J Stonehouse and T Bilton. (Photograph by courtesy of
Kirkleatham Old Hall Museum.)

On Thursday 1st November the *Zetland* was taken by road to Stockton to
take part in a lifeboat procession on the following Saturday. 'Gay with decoration
it will be sure to attract much notice, being the oldest lifeboat in the world.'

1895

The *Zetland* was paraded through the streets of Middlesbrough as one of the
Lifeboat Saturday attractions on the 22nd June. The procession was over a mile
long and also included the Seaton Carew lifeboat *John Lawson.*

An unfortunate mishap overtook the *Zetland* on her way back to Redcar and was reported in 'Northern Notes' of the *North Eastern Daily Gazette* on the 25th June:

'The old Redcar lifeboat, which has been famed in song and in story, and which was on exhibition at the Middlesbrough demonstration on Saturday last, has not reached its destination yet. It started on its homeward journey on Saturday evening, and was dragged along by half a dozen powerful horses. When it got on to the level road between Ormesby and Normanby one of the large back wheels gave way, and the boat and the heavy iron frame were precipitated into the middle of the road from whence no human power could move them. There they lie. Late travellers last night saw the boat and the watchers in their great oilskin coats keeping guard. It is a curious fate that has wrecked the gallant old *Zetland* on land after she had braved so many storms on the ocean.'

No account has yet been found of how or when the *Zetland* was returned to Redcar, but an entry in RNLI records states: ' The carriage of the old private lifeboat which was nearly 100 years old broke down and the men to whom the boat belonged requested the Institution to give them 4 front wheels to enable them to provide a trolley for their boat. The Institution complied with their request.'

1897

An extended version was produced of the information by An Old Stager (first published in the *Redcar and Saltburn-by-the-Sea Gazette* in 1894). The work has come to be known as 'The *Zetland* Lifeboat Log' and copies have survived through generations of families whose names are inextricably linked with the *Zetland* and the history of Redcar. The identities of An Old Stager and the author of the extended history remain unknown and may have been the same person.

What has survived are errors that have been repeated in good faith down the years. An Old Stager claimed that 'on the 7th October, 1802, the famous lifeboat built by Greathead, arrived at Redcar, and was joyously re-christened "*Zetland*". For two years previously she was stationed at Spurn Point, near the mouth of the Humber'. The claim was repeated in the 1897 version.

That the *Zetland* was built in 1802 and not 1800 has been confirmed by contemporary accounts and a list prepared by Henry Greathead of the lifeboats he had built. Therefore it is impossible for the lifeboat to have been stationed at Spurn Point before 1802. In the columns of a York newspaper for 1802 there were suggestions for a lifeboat to be placed at the mouth of the Humber. Greathead read of the proposals and wrote to Trinity House of Hull with an offer to build a lifeboat. The difficulty was in finding sufficient men to form a

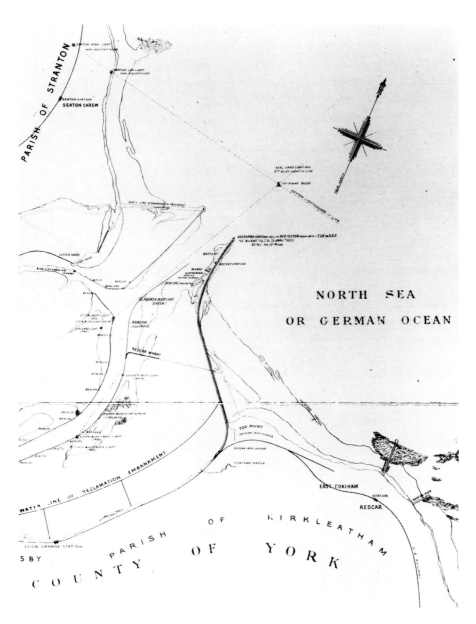

*A chart of the Tees produced in 1897 by the Tees Conservancy
Commissioners. The construction of the South Gare breakwater (named
South Pier on the chart) completely altered the geography of the estuary. At
low-water ordinary spring tides, the depth of water at the entrance had been
increased to about 18 feet (5.5m). (Chart by courtesy of the Tees and
Hartlepool Port Authority.)*

crew. Spurn Point would have provided an ideal site but it was an isolated peninsular and its remoteness offered no form of employment. Consequently it had no community from which a crew could be formed. The situation was not resolved until 1810 when an order was placed with Greathead. Thus the first moves towards a lifeboat at Spurn Point were not made until two years after the *Zetland* was supposed to have been sent there.

The claim that the lifeboat was 'joyously re-christened *Zetland*' on her arrival at Redcar would also seem to be erroneous. It is generally accepted that the name was to honour the lord of the manor who had placed the order for the boat and had paid for a boathouse to be built on land that he had given. Grateful though his tenants and others undoubtedly were the name Zetland (an alternative to Shetland) was unlikely to have had any significance for them.

The benevolent gentleman was Baron Dundas of Aske, a title he held until his death on the 14th June 1820. The title Earl of Zetland was not created until 1838 and was bestowed upon his son, Lawrence, on the 2nd July, less than a week after the coronation of Queen Victoria.

The first contemporary reference to the boat having the name *Zetland* would seem to have been in 1871. Earlier accounts refer only to 'the lifeboat', or in later years 'the old lifeboat'. After such a lapse of time it is unlikely to be discovered when the name was given.

The 1897 account claimed that the *Zetland* had saved 'upwards of 500 lives from a watery grave'. The rescue from the *Luna* on the 29th October 1880 brought the known number of calls answered, whether successful or not, to seventy-seven and the known number of lives saved to either 416 or 441. The alternative totals are the result of conflicting accounts as to the numbers saved from a sloop (1807), the *Caledonia* (1808), the *Rifleman* (1817), and the *Jane Erskine* (1854). In addition there were at least eight occasions when the number saved was not recorded. A generous estimate of ten for each rescue would increase the total to almost 500.

1899

The *Redcar and Saltburn-by-the-Sea Gazette* reported on the 30th September: 'One of the Redcar lifeboats, which is to take part in the procession at Middlesbrough, left Redcar on Thursday afternoon, resting on its own carriage drawn by a traction engine. This boat named "The Zetland" is of the most primitive kind, and shows a great contrast to the present up-to-date boats with their many improvements.'

1900-1909

1901

On the 21st September the *Zetland* was included in the procession on Middlesbrough Lifeboat Day. It was a spectacular event that was the culmination of several fundraising activities in the area. The procession, in four sections, was headed by the Cleveland Steel Works Prize Silver Band and proceeded along the principal streets of Middlesbrough.

The second section was headed by the North Yorks Artillery Volunteer Band and included an RNLI lifeboat (possibly the *Brothers* from Redcar), soldiers of the Yorkshire Hussars, a carriage with the president Col S A Sadler M P, and his wife and party, the Cleveland Hunt, and Royal Navy personnel with a quick-firing nine-pounder field gun used in the battle of Tel-el-Kebir.

The *Zetland* was in the third section and was preceded by a bugle band, a quick-firing Colt gun with a Dundonald galloping carriage, yeomanry returned from the Boer War, acting service volunteers, carriages with the mayor, deputy mayor, and members of the Corporation and officials, and members of the Middlesbrough fire brigade. The fourth section was made up of decorated floats, bands and representatives from many local trades and organisations.

1904

The 1st September. Minute of Redcar Local Board:
'Old Life-Boat *Zetland*
A letter was read from Mr Meek respecting the removal of the old life-boat. Moved by the chairman, seconded by councillor Baker and carried unanimously that the letter be received and a copy thereof entered on the minutes:
"Dear sir,
The old *Zetland* Lifeboat in the brick shed at the South end of the Esplanade will have to be moved soon on account of the extension and it has been suggested

Kitty Sill. Redcar. England.

The Old Lifeboat, "Zetland."
Built by Henry Greathead, of South Shields, in 1800, and placed at Redcar on the 7th October, 1802. Was in active service for 62 years, and was instrumental in saving over 500 lives. Believed to be the oldest lifeboat in the world.

This photograph, taken by T H Nelson, was used again for a postcard that also showed the new shelter proposed for the Zetland in 1905. (From a postcard in a private collection.)

that it should be placed in a building on the Esplanade somewhere opposite the RN lifeboat house so as to be an ornament and an addition to the attractions of the place besides forming a shelter. At a meeting of the committee of Management of the Boat of which Mr. Nelson is chairman and myself secretary I was requested to write and invite the co-operation of the Urban District Council either by undertaking the matter as a Council or deputing some of their members to act with the Committee. I may add that Lord Zetland has promised £50 towards the expense.

Yours very truly
J M Meek."

Appointment of Committee.

Moved by Councillor Hill, seconded by Councillor Storrow and carried unanimously that a committee consisting of the Chairman and Councillors Baker, Hudson, Phillipson, Walker, and Wardman be appointed to act with the Committee in endeavouring to find a suitable place for the Old Life-Boat.

Signed John Bulmer,
chairman.'

1st October, *Redcar and Saltburn News*:

'The Committee for providing a house in which to locate the Old Redcar Life-Boat met a few days ago with the object of finding a site for the same. They hit upon one or two likely spots, but it is not an easy matter to procure that which would best serve the purpose. One of the places chosen was the site at the end of Clarendon Terrace in High Street and this would be an admirable position if it could be secured. The piece of land was leased by the late Mr H Harrison to prevent the sea view from his house opposite being obscured, but probably a one storied erection would not obstruct the sea view from the house opposite.'

31st December, *Redcar and Saltburn News*:

'The selected site for the shelter of the Old Life-Boat the "*Zetland*" is on the Esplanade about opposite the Swan Hotel. To carry out the scheme between £300 and £400 will be needed which will require a big effort to raise. Lord Zetland has promised £50 and it is expected that others will subscribe liberally. If the suggested shelter could be combined with the house perhaps the Council could aid the scheme financially.'

1905

On the 16th May Mr Meek again met with the council with regard to shelter for the *Zetland* and asked them to assist. It was moved by Councillor Phillipson, seconded by Councillor Robson, and carried unanimously that the matter be referred to the works committee for consideration.

19th August, *Redcar and Saltburn News*:

'Efforts are being made to secure sufficient money for the new house for the old lifeboat on the Esplanade. A postcard has been published showing the old boat and the house intended to be erected. The design is a very neat one and it is very pleasing to learn that the old boat which is endeared to the Redcar fishermen will find a home worthy of its tradition.'

The *Newcastle Daily Journal* included a history of the *Zetland* and commented: ' At Redcar, practically homeless and destitute, the oldest lifeboat in the world may be seen - a relic of north country ingenuity, humanitarianism, enterprise, and heroism.' The *London Daily Graphic* for the 9th September also included an article about the boat.

A meeting of Redcar Urban District Council was held on Thursday the 2nd November and 'confirmed the spending of £250 on shelters around the new lifeboat house'. The resolution was rescinded at a meeting on the 16th November when the clerk stated that the voting of the money for the shelters had been illegal.

1906

At some time, the *Zetland* was removed to Marske and reputedly stored in the old granary yard. It would seem that a trust or committee was formed to care for her. About £280 was collected and the *Free Gardeners* lifeboathouse was purchased.

It had been built in 1877 and had included a residence for 'the keeper of the boat', a committee room, reading room, and observatory. Mrs Emma Dawson, of Weston Hall, Otley, had given £100 towards the construction of the boathouse. For many years she and her entourage had stayed in Redcar during the summer season.

She had taken a great interest in the town and had been a generous friend to the inhabitants, particularly the fishermen. At a ceremony in 1877 she had officially named the lifeboat *United Free Gardener*, but it had generally been referred to with affection as the *Emma*. Mrs Dawson died at Weston Hall on the 29th October 1880, the day after the great gale. She may not have been aware that the lifeboat had succeeded in another rescue on the preceding day.

The *Free Gardeners* lifeboat would seem to have fallen into disuse sometime after 1884. Mrs Dawson had volunteered financial support for it only a short while before her death and her son, Captain Dawson, would seem to have honoured the promise. In 1887 he offered the boat to the RNLI but the offer was declined.

When the steam collier *Rowan* went ashore late on the evening of the 14th April 1893, the coxswain of the RNLI lifeboat, *Brothers*, was at the Tees engaged in pilotage. In his absence the lifeboat was launched under the command of R Picknett and J Thompson. An account of the rescue in the *Redcar and Saltburn News* refers to them as 'the two former coxswains of the now defunct United Free Gardeners lifeboat'.

Five years later the *Free Gardeners* Lifeboat was launched in a vain attempt to rescue the crew of the Finnish barque *Birger* in a terrific storm on the 18th October 1898. The oars must have deteriorated with years of disuse for they had broken and the crew were lucky to escape with their lives as the lifeboat was driven between the piles of Coatham pier.

Records have not survived in the archives of the United Free Gardeners but it would seem that the lifeboat was sold to someone in Hartlepool, possibly to leave the boathouse vacant for the *Zetland*

A photo produced by H W Sellars, stationers of Redcar, shows the *Zetland* outside Marske Hall. *(See page 7.)* It is believed to have been taken on the day of her triumphant return to Redcar. The hall was the former residence of Lord Zetland and later Henry Yeoman Walker.

18th August, *Redcar and Saltburn News*:

'The old Redcar lifeboat has now been safely housed in the building provided on the Esplanade. A tablet has been fixed on the boat with the words "Built in 1802, has saved 500 lives, Thine age shall be respected." These simple words tell their own story and show the affection the Redcar fishermen have for the old boat. - OBSERVER.'

*Saltscar at low water. At high water it and the other rocks at Redcar are
completely covered. Their hidden hazard has caused the loss of many ships.
The victim in this instance is the paddle tug* Saxon Prince *which ran aground
on 15th July 1907 and later became a total wreck. Such incidents provided a
welcome bonus for local photographers such as J Boak who took this
photograph. There was a ready demand for prints and postcards from
townsfolk and visitors. (From a postcard in a private collection.)*

1907

On Whit Monday, 20th May, the doors of the former Free Gardeners
lifeboathouse were opened so that the public could view the *Zetland*. From that
date the fortunes of the old boat and the lifeboathouse were to be inextricably
linked, despite several attempts to separate them.

During August, William Dobson died at the age of ninety-two. He had worked
for Lord Zetland for fifty years and had been a member of the crew of the
Zetland. In February 1898 he had been presented with an oil painting of himself
'in *Zetland* crew uniform' painted by Mr Woodhouse of Morecambe. The

painting was reproduced in *The Book of the Lifeboat* and entitled 'The Lifeboatman'.

1909

Articles continued to be written about the *Zetland*, and one in the *Redcar and Saltburn News* of the 19th June concluded:

'But the old salts of Redcar and district yet doubt if the newer boats are equal to this one for many things, and shake their heads doubtfully. To them there can never be any other boat like the *Zetland* and it must be admitted that these fishermen are sailors who ought to know.'

1910-1919

The years between 1910 and 1919 were uneventful for the *Zetland* as its fortunes were overshadowed by the horrors of the First World War. Redcar was crowded by young servicemen. Soldiers completing their training before going to France were billeted in and around the town and a flying field for the Royal Naval Air Service was built on part of the racecourse and nearby farmland. Regular patrols were flown over the North Sea to seek predatory U boats and at night their quarry was that equally sinister terror weapon — the Zeppelin. For a while the pride in the past was replaced by a fear of the future.

1920-1929

1920

8th April. The minutes of Redcar Urban District Council recorded that a vellum and silver ink-stand had been presented to Mr J Meek on his retirement as honorary secretary of the Redcar lifeboat. He had held office for thirty-seven years, during which time there had been three lifeboats, and a total of 150 lives had been saved. Reference was made to his efforts 'to preserve the old lifeboat as a possession of the town'.

1924

7th April. At a meeting of Redcar Urban District Council a letter from Mr J M Meek was read suggesting that the corporation should take over the control and maintenance of the old *Zetland* lifeboathouse on the Esplanade. The mayor (Alderman B O Davies, who was also chairman of the meeting) was asked to discuss this matter with Mr Meek, one of the original trustees, and to raise the matter at a future meeting.

1925

Minutes of the general purposes committee of RUDC.

14th May. 'Mr Meek, on behalf of the trustees of the old Zetland lifeboat, handed over the deeds of the lifeboathouse on the Esplanade together with the old lifeboat itself, and on the motion of the Mayor (Alderman B O Davies), seconded by Ald. Wardman, it was ordered :- "that the town council undertake the future maintenance of the old lifeboat and boathouse".'

25th June. 'The committee have gratefully accepted the offer of several gifts for the Old Life-Boat House, and are prepared to receive still more.'

29th September. 'Authority has been given to the chairman of the committee (Coun. Senior) to enter into an arrangement with Mr W Upton, a former coxswain of the lifeboat, to undertake the care of the old Zetland lifeboat and the cleaning of the windows at the lifeboathouse on the payment of £5 per annum.'

1927

The council paid £7 10s (£7.50) for an attendant for the museum. Between 1928 and 1935 the rate was reduced to £5 for each year, and for 1937 and 1938 the rate was only £2 10s (£2.50) per year.

1928

2nd October, minutes of the Sands Committee.

'There was laid before the committee a statement showing the income and expenditure at the old Zetland lifeboathouse, where Councillor Robinson has undertaken to create a little museum. The committee approved the idea of a portion of the balance of £8.16.8 [approx £8.85] being donated to the renovation of the headstone of William Guy, a pilot who lost his life in an attempt to render assistance to the crew of a Danish vessel off Redcar on Christmas day 92 years ago. The committee desire to express appreciation of the keen interest which Coun. Robinson is taking in the old lifeboat and in the promotion of a miniature museum.'

Appreciation was twice more expressed, and on 5th January 1931 it was minuted that Dr A S Robinson had accepted the position of honorary curator for the museum on the Esplanade.

Dr Alfred Skirrow Robinson was one of Redcar's general practitioners at a time when the town was small enough for him to do his rounds on a bicycle. He had come from Leeds as a young doctor and soon became established as a popular member of the community. His public spirit led him to be chairman of the Redcar branch of the RNLI and a councillor with Redcar Urban District Council, a post from which he resigned in 1930 after seven years service. In 1921 he loaned the council £1,120 to buy a fire engine and £1,064 to buy a steamroller.

1930-1939

1931

On Tuesday 5th April, Mr H J Polden and members of the Polden family visited the *Zetland* in the company of Capt J T Shaw, the honorary secretary of Redcar Lifeboat station.

At a ceremony on the Esplanade during the previous afternoon Mr Polden, on behalf of the trustees and members of the family, had presented a new motor lifeboat, the first to be stationed at Redcar. The lifeboat had been a gift to the RNLI of the late J J Polden of Grove Park, Kent, and members of his family. His daughter, Mrs K M Reeves, had officially christened the lifeboat *Louisa Polden*.

1935

6th April, *Cleveland Standard*.
    'Last Link With Old Zetland Broken.
    Many Mourners At Picknett Funeral.

Mr Thomas Hood Picknett was united with two sons and a brother whom he had lost over thirty years ago in a wreck which he himself survived when on Saturday he was buried in the same grave. His wife, who died a short while ago, is also buried in the family grave at Redcar Cemetery.

Mr. Picknett died two months short of his 89th birthday and was the oldest of three or four generations of the family which were represented at his funeral. His funeral service was conducted in Redcar Parish Church by the Rev H Robson, vicar of Redcar.

It was attended by members of all the old Redcar fishing families and representatives of the Teesmouth and Redcar lifeboats, the Coastguard Service and many other organisations. Mr. Picknett was the last surviving member of the old Zetland lifeboat.'

Thomas Hood Picknett had died at the old lifeboathouse on the 26th March. He had always had a great pride in the *Zetland*. His first lifeboat trip had been

The Free Gardeners *lifeboathouse, where Thomas Hood Picknett lived, is now the* Zetland *Lifeboat Museum. It is pictured here with flags flying for carnival week 1984. Since 1981 the volunteer committee and helpers have ensured that the museum has been open regularly during the summer months so that visitors could see the* Zetland. *Their tireless efforts have also raised thousands of pounds for the RNLI. (Photograph by courtesy of Jane Foreman.)*

as a member of her crew on that momentous occasion in February 1864 when she had been damaged whilst rescuing the crew of the brig *Brothers*. It had been the start of a long association with lifeboats at Redcar, particularly that of the Free Gardeners. Records suggest that he and his wife, Mary, had lived and brought up their family in the accommodation over the Free Gardeners lifeboathouse from the time it was built, a period of almost fifty-eight years.

16th July. Sir Godfrey Baring, Bart, chairman of the committee of management of the RNLI, was shown the *Zetland* and signed the museum visitors' book. He had been guest of honour at a garden party given by Dr Robinson, chairman of the Redcar branch of the RNLI. Other members of the branch committee had also been present. At Whitby, a few days earlier, Sir

Godfrey had attended the annual meeting of RNLI branch chairmen and honorary secretaries of the North of England.

5th December. The finance committee of Redcar Urban District Council discussed a letter from the executors of the late Thomas Hood Picknett. A sub-committee was requested to inspect the premises over the old lifeboathouse with a view to purchase. Thomas Hood Picknett had been the owner of the lease.

1936

Further negotiations by the council led to the purchase of the premises above the old lifeboathouse which were accessible from 5 King Street. £300 was paid for the leasehold to the executors of Thomas Hood Picknett and £1,025 to the Zetland Estate Company for the freehold reversion.

On the 2nd July, the town clerk reported to the finance committee that he had spoken with the mayor (John William Farren) and Dr Robinson about the premises and that repairs were needed to the total of £18 5s (£18.25). H Guy had been appointed caretaker of the old lifeboathouse.

1937

On the 15th March, Dr Robinson gave a talk about the *Zetland* in the Albion Terrace Methodist schoolroom, Saltburn. Dr E J Burnett presided and said of Dr Robinson that he 'was a very fitting person to give the lecture as he had been the man who had rescued the old boat and got it housed'. Dr Robinson recounted how Dr McKinley and Messrs Meek and Groves, together with others, had taken charge of the *Zetland* and formed a trust.

Care had been handed to him and he had looked after it ever since. He went on to outline the history of the *Zetland* and described the loss of William Guy on Christmas Day 1836. Guy had been buried in Redcar churchyard and Dr Robinson told his audience 'that all the pennies that were gained through those who entered the museum were being used to restore the tombstone which is in a state of decay'.

He told of how the government had formed a National Maritime Museum which was to be opened the following month by the king. The new museum was looking for objects of outstanding interest and had negotiated with him in order to get the *Zetland*. He assured his audience that 'you can take it from me they won't get it'. (An entry in the visitors book of the *Zetland* museum shows that George P B Naish of the National Maritime Museum visited on the 11th August 1936.)

Dr Robinson illustrated his talk with a model of the *Zetland* and several pictures and artefacts. Amongst them was the lifeboat drum and a silver tankard that had been presented to George Robinson, one of the steersmen of the *Zetland* for a rescue he had performed in May 1834. The tankard had been passed down to his grandson, William Dixon, of Henry Street, Redcar, who had loaned it for the lecture. The Rev J Toyn, secretary of the Saltburnian Association, thanked Dr Robinson for his talk.

An article was published in the *Evening Gazette* headed 'Oldest Lifeboat - Station does not want to part with it': 'The authorities at a London Museum are anxious to secure as a national memorial the oldest lifeboat in existence which is the old Zetland at Redcar on the North Yorkshire coast.' A brief history of the *Zetland* was given and the article concluded 'another institution, at Hull, is also keen to secure the old relic but up to now the folk of Redcar are determined not to part with their old friend, the Zetland.'

1938

On the 28th June it was decided by the council that the premises above the old lifeboathouse were to be advertised as a flat at a rent of 15 shillings (75p) a week. The first annual report of Redcar public library commented that 'the museum in the Zetland lifeboathouse continues to attract interest and the attention of many visitors during the year'.

1940-1949

1940

The Second World War brought considerable changes to Redcar, as it did to other coastal towns. The beach and adjacent roads and sand dunes were turned into a fortified line of defence under the jurisdiction of the military authorities. Access to the Esplanade was restricted and the old lifeboathouse became one of a number of attractions that were closed for the duration of the war. Again there was a fear of invasion, as there had been when the *Zetland* had arrived at Redcar almost 140 years earlier.

1st April. At a meeting of the library and museums committee, the borough engineer and borough electrical engineer were requested to report on a suitable means of ventilating and heating the old lifeboathouse, 'to preserve the exhibits therein'.

At a subsequent meeting on the 24th April it was decided that, in response to the report, the number of airbricks would be increased to four and a louvre fitted in the centre of the front transom. The borough electrical engineer was instructed to wire two electrical points for the installation of two tubular heaters at a cost of £8 10s (£8.50) each, 'for the purpose of heating the old boathouse'.

1942

24th March. The town clerk reported to the library and museums committee that he had given consideration to the question of approaching the National Trust with regard to the *Zetland*, and had found that the trust was mainly for the preservation of places of historic interest or natural beauty, and that the Associated Societies and Councils all working in this, did not 'include among their objects any which might possibly include the Zetland'.

It was resolved that the borough engineer be requested to report on the provisioning of a blast wall at the entrance to the old lifeboathouse to protect the *Zetland*, and to suggest what steps should be taken for her general preservation.

The blast wall cost £28 and covered the whole length and height of the glassed entrance from the Esplanade. The borough engineer reported 'that the timber of the lifeboat appeared to be in reasonably sound condition, and adequately protected with paint'. The borough librarian was 'instructed to arrange for the doors and windows of the Lifeboat House to be opened from time to time during the warm weather for ventilation purposes'.

1945

20th February. The town clerk reported to the library and museums committee that Col T K J Ridley, one of the trustees of the estate of the late Dr Robinson, had forwarded a typewritten copy of an 'Epic and Log of the old lifeboat "*Zetland*"' to the librarian. It was resolved that subject to investigation of copyright the log would be printed, bound and placed in the reference library.

Dr Alfred Skirrow Robinson had been killed in the Zetland Club when three high-explosive bombs had fallen on Redcar on the night of the 21st October 1941.

1946

With the end of wartime restrictions, the council gave attention to the restoration of Redcar as a seaside resort.

25th June. At a meeting of the library and museums committee the borough engineer was instructed to remove the blast wall from in front of the old lifeboathouse.

1947

26th February. The library and musuems committee resolved to discuss the reopening of the *Zetland* lifeboat museum.

23rd April. The borough engineer was instructed to inspect the *Zetland* and report on its condition and get expert advice if needed. The borough librarian was to overhaul the museum collection and dispose of such items as were not considered desirable to retain.

26th June. The borough engineer reported that the *Zetland* appeared to need certain repairs and renovation. It was resolved that advice be obtained from a capable boat builder and that a special meeting of the committee be held to make recommendations as to the future care of the *Zetland*. There would seem to be no record of any work being carried out.

During September permission was granted for part of the old lifeboathouse to be used for painting and storing scenery from the New Pavilion.

1949

On the 22nd June a subcommittee of the library and musuems committee was formed to decide on future policy with regard to the old lifeboathouse. The borough engineer was requested to paint the premises as soon as possible and remove white paint that covered the doors and windows.

Over a period of time the dilapidated appearance of the *Zetland* and the boathouse had given rise to letters of criticism in the press. One correspondent complained under the pseudonym 'I came but could not see':

'Its [the *Zetland's*] present appearance and outlook are, to say the least, gloomy and must produce caustic comments from the numerous visitors who attempt, unsuccessfully, to see through the grimy cracked windows of its boathouse.'

On the 14th September the subcommittee met with representatives of the RNLI with regard to opening the old lifeboathouse to the public during the following year. It was agreed that the RNLI should be responsible for staffing. The periods suggested for opening were Whit Week, all June, July and August, possibly part of September, and 'other such times as the RNLI considered proper'.

It was also agreed that the RNLI be allowed a donation box and retain all monies, and that the entertainments and publicity manager be asked to cease using the lifeboathouse as a store for scenery etc.

In October the borough engineer quoted £50 to have the large folding doors onto the Esplanade repaired, and reported that 'the Zetland was in good condition'.

1950-1959

1951

17th October. The library and museums committee again considered future policy with regard to the old lifeboathouse and reference was made to the unsatisfactory condition of the interior. It was decided to defer the matter until January 1952 with a view to setting aside a sum of money in the estimates.

The borough librarian was requested to approach the local branch of the RNLI with a view to keeping the building open for a longer period during the forthcoming season. The town clerk was requested to report upon the possibilities of making a charge for admission or for the sale of pamphlets.

On the 21st November the town clerk reported that an admission charge could not be made as the old lifeboathouse had been acquired under the Public Libraries Act. The money had been borrowed for the purchase of the property for museum purposes and the act provided that no charge for admission could be made to a library or museum.

There was no objection to the sale of pamphlets telling the history of the lifeboat provided that purchase of them was not a condition of admission. At the same meeting a letter was submitted from the secretary of the Redcar branch of the RNLI. He suggested that the supervision of the *Zetland* could be more easily undertaken if the operational lifeboat (*City of Leeds*) and the *Zetland* were housed in one building. It would enhance the interest in both boats and the site suggested was that adjoining the RNLI boathouse.

The scheme was approved in principle by the committee subject to consent from the Ministry of Housing and Local Government to the appropriation of the old lifeboathouse for purposes other than a museum. Like many previous grand schemes, it came to nothing.

1952

The borough librarian was authorised to engage a suitable person to act as attendant at the old lifeboathouse over the Whitsuntide weekend 'and whenever the possibility of custom would appear to warrant it'. Money collected was to be split halfand half between the attendant and the RNLI.

Negotiations began with HM Coastguard with regard to the erection of a look-out on top of the old lifeboathouse.

1955

28th September. The chairman of the library and museums committee commented on the state of the old lifeboathouse after the building of the coastguard look-out. After an inspection it was estimated that it would cost £20 to clean and £40 to decorate. It was also reported that the borough engineer was to take steps to stop damage caused by woodworm to supports beneath the *Zetland*. The damage had been discovered during the inspection.

1959

23rd September. Reference was made to the entertainment committee suggestion that a suitable description and photograph of the old *Zetland* lifeboat be included in the town guide. It was agreed, and 5,000 copies of next year's guide, printed by Sotheran, included this.

1960-1969

1960

16th March. The library and museums committee gave permission to the Ladies Lifeboat Guild to open the old boathouse to raise funds for the RNLI. The guild hoped to develop a maritime museum and suggested that a sign-board over the doorway would help to draw the attention of visitors. The estimated cost of the sign was £25 and authorisation was given for it to be erected.

The *Zetland* was featured on Christmas cards sent by the Mayor and Mayoress, Councillor and Mrs George William Thorne.

1961

25th January. It was reported at a meeting of the library and museums committee that the outside walls of the old lifeboathouse needed to be completely repointed and all exterior woodwork repainted. The large doors onto the Esplanade needed to be repaired, or replaced, and the flat above the boathouse needed new timber floors. The estimated cost of the work was £350.

At the same meeting it was reported that the borough librarian had approached Laurie Picknett with a proposal to compile a film record of the documents and books he owned, with a view to preparing an authentic and informative history of Redcar. A film reader would need to be purchased and a Recordac Industrial Reader was suggested at a cost of £85.

(At a meeting on the 25th January 1962, it was reported that there may be problems with the proposed document copying machine and its ability to photocopy bound volumes, and that a delay in its purchase be recommended. In consequence it seems that Mr Picknett's documents and books were never copied and a wonderful opportunity was lost to put much of the town's history on permanent record.)

19th April. Estimates for new big doors onto the Esplanade were quoted at £98 for softwood, and £125 for hardwood. It was recommended that hardwood

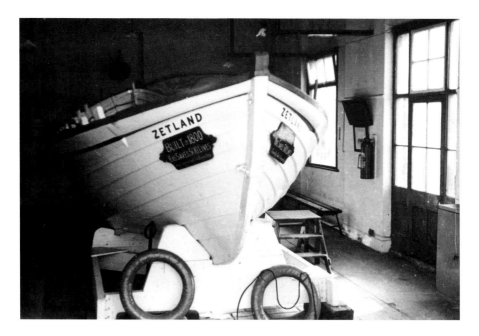

The Zetland *in 1965. During the 1960s the Redcar Ladies Lifeboat Guild had permission from Redcar Borough Council to open the boathouse in the summer for the sale of RNLI souvenirs. (Photograph by the author.)*

doors be fitted and renovation work be done on the front elevation of the boathouse at a total cost of £225.

1962

20th June, the library and museums committee gave consideration to a memorandum of a meeting held on the 16th May with representatives of the RNLI at which suggestions were made for the re-siting of the operational lifeboathouse and the possibility of re-housing the *Zetland*.

Further discussion took place on the 18th July with reference to loaning the *Zetland* to the local committee of the RNLI. Concern was felt that the local committee might cease, and it was agreed by the library and museums committee that the *Zetland* be offered on loan to the main body of the RNLI on the understanding that it remained in Redcar.

23rd July. At a meeting of the finance and general purpose committee the town clerk submitted a letter from A Walker and Son, appointed agent to the

RNLI, with reference to the new lifeboathouse. Three sites were proposed:

(1) Adjacent to the existing lifeboathouse with a widened slipway.

(2) On the east side of Dundas Street slipway.

(3) Between the bandstand and shelter opposite West Terrace.

The RNLI preferred the second option. Provision was to be made for housing the *Zetland* in the new building, the cost of which, with a slipway, would be in the region of £35,000.

The suggestion that the *Zetland* and the operational lifeboat be housed together was a revival of the 1951 proposal. It was the start of many years of negotiation that would outlast Redcar Borough Council. The need for a larger lifeboathouse was necessitated by the introduction of the thirty-seven feet long Oakley class lifeboat as the standard carriage launched lifeboat of the RNLI fleet. The new type was longer, wider and heavier than the self-righting class and the non self-righting Liverpool class that it replaced.

A compromise was finally reached between the newly-formed Teesside Council and the RNLI, but there was no provision for the *Zetland* on the agreed site. The new lifeboathouse was completed in 1972 and officially opened by the Marquess of Zetland on Whit Monday, the 28th May, of the following year.

1963

A small inscribed plate was discovered by Roy Barker, the bowman of the Redcar lifeboat *City of Leeds*, whilst he helped to clean the interior of the *Zetland*. It was on the apron of one of the end posts and had been covered with many layers of paint. When the layers had been removed, the plate was found to bear the inscription 'Invented and constructed by Henry Greathead of South Shields. Contractor for the lifeboats'.

22nd April. At a special meeting of the library and museums committee consideration was given to a letter dated the 19th April from the RNLI. This stated that it proposed to hold an International Lifeboat Conference in Edinburgh in June and that they would like to have the *Zetland* lifeboat on loan as a centrepiece for the exhibition.

The borough librarian reported that one of the institution's inspectors had examined the boat and confirmed that it was in a sound condition. If the council agreed to the request a special cradle would be constructed on which to convey the boat to Edinburgh and every care would be taken during transportation and at the exhibition. The committee agreed to the request.

Fog hung over the coast on Friday the 31st May as the *Zetland* was eased out of her boathouse and placed on a low-bed trailer. The occasion attracted a large crowd and was recorded by members of the Redcar Amateur Ciné Club.

Offshore, the fog caused ships to move cautiously about the Tees estuary and delayed the arrival of a new lifeboat of the South Holland Lifeboat Society. It

The Zetland *being taken from her boathouse on the 31st May 1963, prior to being taken to Leith to be exhibited at the Ninth International Lifeboat Conference. The front doors of the building had to be completely removed and can be seen at the side. (Photograph by courtesy of the* Evening Gazette.*)*

was to pay a courtesy visit to the Teesmouth lifeboat station before going north to be part of the International Lifeboat Conference.

The conference was held in Edinburgh and was attended by delegates from nineteen countries. At the nearby port of Leith they had the opportunity to inspect and go to sea in ten of the most up to date lifeboats in the world. Five belonged to the RNLI and five to other countries.

The *Zetland* was exhibited in a marquee on the quayside and attracted long queues of interested people eager to view and go on board. Redcar historian Laurie Picknett had accompanied the boat to answer questions and guarantee her safekeeping. Amongst the distinguished visitors he met was Princess Marina, President of the RNLI, who remarked: 'I think she is a wonderful old boat and you must be very proud of her'.

The return journey to Redcar began on Friday the 7th June. An overnight stay was made at Alnwick where the *Zetland* was too wide for an archway in

The Zetland *in the exhibition marquee at Leith for the Ninth International Lifeboat Conference in 1963. She was a great contrast to the modern lifeboats moored in the harbour close by. (Photograph by courtesy of Jack Fisher, Edinburgh.)*

the main street and a detour had to be made. It was carnival week and earnest pleas were made by the townsfolk for the boat to remain there for the Saturday celebrations. Unfortunately it was not possible.

At Easington a halt was made and the *Zetland* was dressed overall for the remainder of the journey to Redcar. Upon her safe return Laurie Picknett paid tribute to lorry driver Bill Hill, of Hartlepool, for his skill in handling such an unusual load. He also told of how the *Zetland* had created great interest in every town and village she had passed through.

19th June. A letter of thanks from the RNLI for the loan of the *Zetland* was read at a meeting of the library and museums committee. The Ladies Lifeboat Guild indicated that the interior of the *Zetland* needed painting as a result of the number of people that had been on board at Edinburgh. The committee resolved to write to the RNLI for special paint for conservation.

A reply was read at a subsequent meeting to the effect that the RNLI used no special paint for conservation but was willing to supply paint as used on their own lifeboats. Mr T B Picknett (former coxswain of the Redcar lifeboat *City of Leeds*) had offered to do the work. The committee accepted both offers.

1967

On Friday the 30th June, Richard Laurence 'Laurie' Picknett died at his home at the age of sixty-four. He had been a partner in the fishmongers that carried the family name and an enthusiastic local historian. For many years he had given talks on old Redcar and done much to promote interest in the *Zetland*. He had also done considerable work for the League of Friends of Stead Hospital and was president for the year at the time of his death.

1968

Under local government reorganisation, part of North Yorkshire, including Redcar, and part of county Durham were absorbed into the newly created County Borough of Teesside.

The amalgamation produced a large museum service with greater resources. For the first time the old lifeboathouse was opened on a regular basis with full-time staff. A gallery was created in the former living accommodation upstairs and the area around the *Zetland* was redisplayed with photographs and items of local interest. Amongst the latter were some that had been on show for more than thirty years. They included the stern board of a ship obtained by Dr Robinson and used by him for a while as part of a hen coop, the figurehead from the *England's Rose* wrecked at Redcar in 1876, and a plaque commemorating the loss of William Guy on Christmas Day 1836.

A small downstairs room was converted to represent a fisherman's baithouse and for the first time the building was given an official name - 'Redcar Shipping and Fishing Museum'. The museum opened its doors to the public on Saturday the 4th October 1969, and attracted 300 visitors. An entry in the day-to-day log stated:'Visitors, particularly old residents, showed great enthusiasm and several offers of exhibits and photographs were received.'

1970 TO THE PRESENT DAY

1974

Further reorganization of local government replaced the County Borough of Teesside with Cleveland County, which in turn was divided into four separate districts. Three took the names of the principal towns in their area - Hartlepool, Stockton and Middlesbrough. The exception was the area south of the Tees which was given the unusual name of Borough of Langbaurgh and extended so as to take in more of North Yorkshire.

The *Zetland* came under the care of Langbaurgh Borough Council Museum Service, and on the 15th May 1975 the Redcar Museum of Shipping and Fishing was renamed Zetland Museum.

Almost 2,000 schoolchildren in organised parties visited the museum each year. They were given conducted tours by a dedicated staff of two attendants, who also dealt with thousands of visitors including a great many from overseas.

1975

A hull inspector from the RNLI made a routine inspection of the *Zetland* on the 20th January. He adopted the customary practise for testing a wooden hulled boat and prodded the planks with a pocket knife. Despite their age, the most recent repair having been made more than a century earlier, they were so hard that they caused the knife to close unexpectedly on his hand!

On the 27th June a marine aquarium was established at the museum to exhibit local examples of sealife. It quickly became a popular attraction and was well supported by Redcar fishermen who kept it stocked with unusual specimens.

1976

A $^1/24$th scale plan of the *Zetland* was drawn by D Phillipson and copies were produced by the museum service to sell as souvenirs.

The Zetland in 1979. From 1974 the museum had been the responsibility of the museum service of Langbaurgh Borough Council. The area around the Zetland and a gallery upstairs were redisplayed, a sea-water aquarium was introduced and a large temporary exhibition gallery was created. The museum also included a Tourist Information Centre. In 1981 the council withdrew all staff and closed the museum as part of a museum centralisation scheme. (Photograph by courtesy of Kirkleatham Old Hall Museum.)

1977

The chairman of the RNLI, Major General Ralph H Farrant CB, and the North-East inspector of lifeboats, Lt Alan Tate, visited the museum to see the *Zetland* on the 15th July.

1978

An ultra-violet retarding film was added to the windows of the museum to prevent damage to the paintwork of the *Zetland* and other exhibits by excessive sunlight.

On the 20th October Lt Alan Tate made a return visit to the museum in the company of Vice-Admiral Sir Arthur Hezlet KBE CB DSO DSC DL, chairman

179 years of lifeboat history had passed at Redcar when these lifeboats were brought together on the 18th October 1981. The occasion was the blessing of the lifeboats to celebrate the start of Maritime England Year. It was also a meeting of the first and last regular all-weather lifeboats at Redcar. In 1985 the Sir James Knott was taken away for overhaul and her duties taken over by a relief lifeboat. Later in the year the RNLI decided that from 1986 Redcar would become solely an inshore lifeboat station. The Sir James Knott was later acquired by Langbaurgh-on-Tees Museum Service and is stored at Kirkleatham Old Hall Museum. (Photograph by the author.)

of the search and rescue committee of the RNLI, Commander D B Cairns RD RNR, chief of operations, and Commander F R H Swann CBE RNVR. (Commander Swann had visited the museum on the 3rd May 1973 during his period of office as chairman of the RNLI.)

1980

Langbaurgh Council revealed plans to centralise the museum service at Kirkleatham Old Hall on the outskirts of Redcar. The scheme included the closure of the Chapel Beck gallery at Guisborough and the Zetland Museum at

Redcar. For a while the future of the *Zetland* seemed uncertain and there was even talk of moving her from her resting place of more than seventy years.

An outraged public rallied to the aid of the old boat. At a crowded public meeting held at the Mayfair public house on the 13th October, an action committee was elected and adopted the name '*Zetland* Lifeboat Savers Association'. Chairman was the coxswain of Redcar lifeboat, David Buckworth, secretary was Redcar businessman Philip Chisholm, and press officer was Ray Preston.

A petition of more than 5,000 names in support of the museum was delivered to the council, and local newspapers received scores of letters in protest against the closure.

1981

Throughout the country, preparations were being made for Maritime England Year organised by the English Tourist Board. Organisations and individuals contributed to a huge calender of events that covered every aspect of maritime heritage. It would have been an ideal opportunity to promote the *Zetland* as a major attraction. Instead the Zetland Museum closed on the 31st March, despite a storm of local protest.

An appeal was made to the RNLI to intervene and officials met with representatives of the council and members of the *Zetland* Lifeboat Savers Association. The RNLI was represented by public relations officer Ray Kipling, and the organising secretary for the North-East district, Ken Thirlwell. After negotiation it was agreed that the RNLI would lease the museum at a peppercorn rent and staff it with volunteers.

At a meeting held in the Park Hotel on the 2nd March, the *Zetland* Lifeboat Savers Association was disbanded and the RNLI Zetland Museum Committee was formed. David Buckworth was elected chairman, Philip Chisholm secretary, David Phillipson honorary curator, and Ray Preston press officer. The nucleus of willing volunteers quickly grew and the museum opened its doors to the public on the 18th May. It continued to be the success it had been under council administration and when it closed for the winter, on the 30th September, it had attracted 13,000 visitors.

At 2pm on Sunday the 18th October, a blessing of the lifeboats was held to celebrate the start of Maritime England Year. The big front doors of Zetland Museum were opened and the operational lifeboat, *Sir James Knott*, was brought along the Esplanade and parked outside. The two lifeboats, old and new, stood only a few feet apart.

A service of thanksgiving for the RNLI and all lifeboat crews was conducted by the Rev Andrew Huckett, chaplain at the Missions to Seamen. Also present were the Rev Rex Whitta, vicar of St Peters Church, and the Rev Martin Amery of the Methodist church. Amongst those that attended the service were the mayor and mayoress, members of the RNLI Zetland Museum committee, representatives of the Redcar and Teesmouth lifeboat crews and members of the Redcar Ladies Lifeboat Guild. The service on the Esplanade was followed by a short service in St Peters Church.

1982

The *Zetland* featured in *The Past Afloat*, a BBC TV series linked with Maritime England Year.

On the 7th October the committee of volunteers organised a social evening at the museum to celebrate the 180th anniversary of the arrival of the *Zetland* at Redcar. Guest of honour was the Marquess of Zetland who presented prizes to the winners of a schools competition. The Mayor of Langbaurgh Borough Council also attended.

15th December. After a period of very cold weather a water pipe burst in the coastguard look-out above the museum. Water poured through the ceiling into the main upstairs gallery and saturated the carpet tiles. It soaked through to the boathouse below and cascaded into the *Zetland*. The walls streamed with water and a hurried rescue operation was mounted to save the displays of photographs.

Langbaurgh Borough Council provided three industrial heaters and the majority of harmful moisture was soon dispersed. Fortunately the *Zetland* came through the ordeal unscathed.

It took many weeks for the volunteers to clean up and re-decorate, but when the museum opened in the following spring there were few signs that the calamity had taken place.

1982 - 1994

The museum continues to attract many thousands of visitors every year. From the sale of souvenirs and money from collecting boxes it has been possible to make regular and substantial donations to the RNLI. In this manner the *Zetland* continues to save life.

The enthusiasm and dedication of the volunteers has never diminished and has been the inspiration for others to follow on. The *Zetland* symbolises the spirit of Redcar, and with care and affection can look forward to her 200th anniversary and beyond.

Bibliography

Baines Yorkshire, Volume II, 1823. Reprinted by David and Charles in 1969.

Bates, G F, *Guide to Redcar and Saltburn-by-the-Sea*. G F Bates, 2nd edition, 1871.

Brewster, J, *The Parochial History and Antiquities of Stockton-upon-Tees*, 1769, second edition 1829.

Census returns; 1841, 1851, 1861, 1871, 1881, 1891.

Cleveland Standard.

Coulson, J and S, and Picknett, W, 'A Journal of Shipwrecks kept at Redcar by Stephen and John Coulson of Redcar from September 1825 to October 1858, continued until 1888 by a copy of a record kept by William Picknett'.

Cowley, Bill, 'Bill Cowley's Yorkshire', *Dalesman*, February 1968.

Dibdin, J C, and Ayling, J, *The Book of the Lifeboat*, Oliphant, Anderson and Ferrier, 1894.

Durham and Northumberland, Volumes I and II, 1827.

Evening Gazette.

Farr, Grahame, *Non Self-righting Pulling and Sailing Lifeboats 1775-1916*, G Farr, 1983.

Farr, Grahame, *Self-righting Pulling and Sailing Lifeboats 1851-1918*, G Farr, 1983.

Farr, Grahame, *George Palmer's Lifeboats 1828-1847*, G Farr, 1975.

Ferguson, D, *The Natural History of Redcar and its Neighbourhood*. Simpkin Marshall, Redcar, J H Webster, 1860.

Gordon, Samuel, *The Watering Places of Cleveland; Being Descriptions of These and Other Attractive Localities in that Interesting District of Yorkshire*. J H Webster, 1869.

History, Topography and Directory of North Yorkshire, T Bulmer and Co, 1890.

Humble, A F, *The Rowing Life Boats of Whitby*. Horne and Son Ltd, 1974.

Hutton, W, *A Trip to Coatham; A Watering Place in the North Extremity of Yorkshire*, John Nichols and Son, 1810.

Kirkleatham Local Board, minutes of meetings.

Langbaurgh Borough Council, minutes of meetings.

Naval Magazine and *Naval Chronicle*, 1837.

Newcastle Chronicle.

Newcastle Courant.

North Eastern Daily Gazette.

Ord, J W, *The History and Antiquities of Cleveland*, Simpkin and Marshall, 1846.

Pattenden, D W, *The Port of Coatham*, Cleveland and Teesside Local History Society Bulletin, December 1970.

Phillipson, D, *Come Along Brave Boys*, Sotheran, 1980.

Redcar and Saltburn-by-the-Sea Gazette.

Redcar and Saltburn News.

Redcar Local Board, minutes of meetings.

Redcar Urban District Council, minutes of meetings.

Richmond, Thomas, *The Local Records of Stockton and the Neighbourhood*, Wm Robinson, 1868. Reprinted by Patrick and Shotton, 1972.

Scoresby, W, *The Loss of the Esk and Lively, Greenland Whalers.* Published to raise funds for the dependants by R Rogers, 1826.

Sykes, J, *Local Records of Northumberland*, Volume 2, 1866. Facsimile copy, Patrick and Shotton 1973.

Teesside County Borough Council, minutes of meetings.

The Lifeboat, published quarterly by the Royal National Lifeboat Institution.

The Redcar Life-Boat Zetland, author unknown, 1897.

Tweddle, G M, *A Visitor's Handbook to Redcar, Coatham and Saltburn.* G M Tweddle, 1850, 2nd edition 1863.

Walbran, J R, *A Visitor's Guide to Redcar*, 1841, 2nd edition 1848.

Walton, P, *Journal Kept on the Coast of Redcar From the Year 1800-1819 by Peter Walton, Officer of the Customs, Stationed at Redcar.* T Jennet of Stockton, 1821.

Warner, O, *The Life-Boat Service, A History of the RNLI 1824-1974*, Cassell, 1974.

Whitaker, Boswell, *Skuetender Lifeboat*, South Tyneside Libraries, 1979.

Whitby Repository and Monthly Miscellany, Volume II, Number 14, February. R Kirby of Whitby, 1826.

York Chronicle.

York Herald.

York Weekly Post.

York Courant.

Yorkshire Gazette.
Zetland Lifeboat Committee accounts and visitor's book commencing Whit
    Monday, 20th May 1907.
Zetland School logbooks.